THE COMPACT GARDEN

THE
COMPACT
GARDEN

DISCOVERING THE PLEASURES
OF PLANTING IN A SMALL SPACE

BRIAN FAWCETT · CAMDEN HOUSE

Canadian Cataloguing in Publication Data

Fawcett, Brian, 1944-
  The compact garden

Includes index.
ISBN 0-921820-43-7

1. Gardening.   I. Title.

SB453.F38 1992   635.9   C92-093448-X

Trade distribution by
Firefly Books
250 Sparks Avenue
Willowdale, Ontario
Canada M2H 2S4

Printed and bound in Canada by
D.W. Friesen & Sons Ltd.
Altona, Manitoba, for
Camden House Publishing
(a division of Telemedia Publishing Inc.)
7 Queen Victoria Road
Camden East, Ontario
K0K 1J0

Design by
Linda J. Menyes

Cover photographs by Rosalind Creasy

Colour separations by
Hadwen Graphics
Ottawa, Ontario

Printed on acid-free paper

□   *ACKNOWLEDGEMENTS*

Thanks go to various gardeners in the neighbourhoods I've lived in over the years. I'd also like to thank Jim Allen, who took the time to read and comment on an early draft of this book. Special thanks go to Nancy Boyd, who was my gardening partner for seven years, during which time the idea for this book was conceived and much of it written.

Thanks also to my editor Tracy Read, for making this project fun, and to the rest of the staff at Camden House: art director Linda Menyes, assistant editor Mary Patton, editorial coordinator Susan Dickinson, photo researcher Jane Good and associates Christine Kulyk, Catherine DeLury, Charlotte DuChene, Laura Elston, Janice McLean and Johanna Troyer.

Thanks of a slightly different kind go to our shrinking population of earthworms that, though blind, deaf and dumb, manage to do more good for the planet than we do.

For my parents, Rita and Hartley Fawcett, who in their different ways made me a gardener.

CONTENTS

COMMON SENSE IN A SMALL SPACE

This downtown garden, left, makes the

most of a small space, incorporating

shade- and sun-loving plants, vegetables,

flowers and a quiet place to sit. The

garden at right has been created literally

upon a layer of concrete.

One afternoon not long ago, a friend asked me to recommend a good gardening book. She had just moved into a house on a small lot a few blocks from me, and she was preparing to do some gardening for the first time in her adult life. The garden in her new backyard was in an advanced state of decay and not really to her taste in any case. Happy to encourage a beginning gardener, I suggested a particular gardening book, saying that it was fairly comprehensive and would cost her more than $40. Then I began to outline the book's strengths and weaknesses.

She listened with a slightly bemused smile to everything I said. "Look," she said at last. "This garden isn't going to be my life's work. All I want to do is grow a few flowers and vegetables. I don't need an *Encyclopaedia Plantannica.*"

My friend was right. Like many housing lots in North American cities, hers is about 30 feet wide and 100 feet deep. Much of it is occupied by the house itself and by such features as sidewalks, a carport and a porch. As a result, the gardening space available is quite limited. In many cities, lot sizes are often even smaller. In fact, many

9

people who have the urge to garden have only a balcony or a small outdoor condominium enclosure with which to work. Gardens in any of these situations share the same basic limitations: they present special problems that arise from lack of space and restricted light.

My friend's gardening intentions were similarly limited. She wanted to putter around a little in her backyard, and she wanted to get something in return—a few tomatoes, perhaps, and some flowers. Eventually, she might begin to experiment with something more elaborate, as most new gardeners do.

Most of the people in North America who garden—or who would like to garden—have a lot more in common with my friend and me than with gardening guru Vita Sackville-West or her legendary colleagues. And when I thought it over, I realized one of the problems was that there just wasn't a gardening book which speaks rationally to the degree of interest people like us usually take in gardening.

I went down to my favourite bookstore and checked out the gardening section. After that, I dropped in at the public library. Not surprisingly, I found hundreds of gardening books. There were books on organic gardening, vegetable gardening, herb gardening, Oriental gardening and flower gardening, gardening with perennials and gardening with annuals.

There were encyclopaedias too. Some were of a general nature, and several were dazzlingly comprehensive—perfectly easy to read if you happen to have a doctorate in horticulture. There were specialized reference books on annuals, perennials, shrubs, trees, vines, bulbs, vegetables, fruit trees and various combinations of the above. There were books on greenhouses and books on how to turn your entire house and garden into an integrated energy-conservation system, bomb shelter and lifestyle outpost. There were some elegant coffee-table books filled with photographs of beautiful garden landscapes

that would stir both envy and hope in the hearts of most gardeners and would-be gardeners, myself included. Many were pretty wonderful, although more than a few were as impractical as they were elegant. A beginner might find them pretty intimidating. And for a beginner to purchase them all, he or she would have to sell the house and ransom the kids.

Nearly all gardening books make what I consider unrealistic assumptions. Some assume that the reader has an unlimited amount of time to garden and an unlimited amount of money and some that the reader owns a property more than an eighth of an acre in size (and frequently much larger). Some assume that the reader has few or no interests other than gardening and some that the reader sees gardening as a spiritual activity leading to purification of the environment or the self. Many books make all those assumptions.

□   MY KIND OF GARDENER

Let me draw a composite portrait of the kind of person who I believe will find this book useful. You're from 15 to 80 years of age. You're male or female, tall to short, slim to heavy. Race, colour and creed are unimportant. You work for a living, or you've got other things to do that prevent you from gardening four to six hours a day in the spring and summer. While you do have some money (and you'll need it, because gardening can be expensive, even on a small scale), it's not sufficient to enable you to hire a crew of gardeners to create your garden for you. (If you do have that much money, you probably don't have the energy or time to enjoy the kind of gardening I will be talking about, and you will probably move out of the neighbourhood soon anyway.)

Ideally, you own the house you're living in, but you certainly don't need to. I gardened steadily during the many years that I rented an apartment or a house. The landlords always loved me for it, and more than once, I saved my-

Ingenuity is often a major player in compact gardening: the cracks in this stone path are home to colourful self-limiting plants, while a wall-hugging, space-saving shrub has established itself beneath the window.

self a rent increase because of the improvements I had made around the place. A couple of times, of course, the opposite happened: I made the premises so appealing that my landlord realized he had a valuable property on his hands and sold it out from under me. Even then, I had the satisfaction of knowing I'd made a small corner of the world a more attractive place.

If you happen to live in a condominium or co-op with bylaws against individual gardens, don't despair. The often stringent and shortsighted rules against anything beyond basic low-upkeep gardening can be changed — and damned well should be. For a year, I lived in a co-op with so many ridiculous restrictions that it almost drove me batty. In return, I drove the co-op landscaping committee crazy, and they did what most threatened bureaucracies do: they created more rules to try to keep me under control. Eventually, I gave up and moved out. But I had started something the committee could not stop. The co-op eventually changed its rules to allow the gardeners among its membership to work their magic. No one there has erected a monument to my pioneering spirit, but whenever I drive by, I see a place where people are able to live and to express, through their gardens, their pleasure in living. Most other such places prefer the landscape to simply look like "developments": thematically correct, sterile and sort of heartless. The co-op I once lived in is a reminder that a determined and creative gardener can utterly transform the spaces he or she has access to.

Like most people these days, I'm very much aware of the profoundly negative impact our culture has had upon our environment, and whenever possible, I try to do something about it. I'd prefer to garden organically, but to be perfectly blunt, modern cities make that very hard to do. Since I live in a city and I'm determined to garden, at times I've had to choose between being pure and having a decent garden.

And so will you, in a variety of sometimes peculiar and innovative ways.

□ *AMATEURS ONLY*

I don't pretend that I'm an expert. I garden partly because I enjoy the activity and partly because I'm literal-minded enough to like to see the results of my labour. I've gardened in climates that are quite friendly to gardeners, and I've gardened in places that weren't friendly at all. I'm what you'd call an experienced amateur with a special interest in restricted spaces. I can provide basic information and a general approach to sensible gardening on a sensible scale. In reading this book, you will also be exposed to a variety of opinions, which I offer for what they're worth and because I can't help myself. All my neighbours have opinions too, as, you will find, do all gardeners. Pay attention to the methods, and enjoy the opinions. Nobody's perfect.

At certain times of the year, I become unreasonably excited about gardening, and it's hard for me to concentrate on anything else. But I fall just short of being what you'd call a passionate gardener. I forget about the garden for days at a time, sometimes weeks. I go away on vacations or business trips, occasionally when my garden desperately needs me to be around. I sometimes fail to harvest crops when they're ready, and the front lawn has sometimes gone uncut for weeks longer than it should. These practices haven't spoiled my garden, and they don't have to spoil yours.

Like the rest of the planet, gardens aren't meant to be perfect. And your garden and gardening habits certainly don't have to be perfect either. You need the confidence to determine your garden's own character as well as access to a few special techniques that will help you transform it into what you want (and have a good time doing it). This book is meant for reasonable, pragmatic souls who have day-to-day duties other than gardening and a wish list of things they don't quite have the time or resources to pursue. I'm writing it because I enjoy gardening. I hope that a sense of the intense pleasure I get from it will pervade these pages and that it will prove to be contagious.

□ *WHY GARDEN?*

Let's begin with the most basic question: Why bother? Gardens are messy, they're filled with dirt, bugs and dead things, and they require care and feeding. If you take them seriously, they're almost as much trouble as kids or pets.

I can think of several very good reasons to garden. First of all, taken in the right spirit, gardening is fun. Fun needs no excuse. If you're not having fun with your garden, there's something wrong with your approach. Second, you will get to know your neighbours, people who, more often than not, have useful opinions and information they are happy to share. You'll find what I've found: there are many more interesting things to talk about with relative strangers than the weather. Third, you will produce fresh, healthful vegetables and beautiful flowers. In a small way, you'll be reducing resource consumption and garbage production, and you'll be helping to supply the planet with a little oxygen. In the ecologists' phrase, you'll become part of the solution rather than part of the problem. Fourth, you'll be involved in some nonroutine outdoor exercise and will thereby improve your mental and physical health. Fifth, you will experience a continuing aesthetic pleasure and the pride of accomplishment.

Finally, let's be practical—and realistic. In restricted spaces, gardening is usually something you do essentially for pleasure. I think of it as an encounter with intangibles, which, I imagine, is why it is probably a more rewarding pastime than, say, amateur accountancy.

□ *WHAT COMPACT GARDENS ARE ALL ABOUT*

Gardening in a restricted space isn't going to be like gardening on an acreage, where you can divide the garden into organized segments, each to fulfill a separate task. In restricted urban spaces, you will find these same elements—and quite a few more—all combined in a single spot. Common sense will tell you that there are things you cannot do and plants you cannot or should not grow. The smaller the gardening space, the fewer options are open to you. While money can solve some of your problems, you are going to have to exercise a different kind of intelligence.

The first thing you ought to do is make an inventory of your entire property. How much of it do you actually control, and how much of it is permanent? In the "permanent" category are fixtures like driveways, garages, sheds, decks, patios, fences, trees, driveway exits to the street, adjoining or attached buildings, power lines (above or below ground), sidewalks, taps, heat pumps, dryer exhausts, windows and doors. Some situations can't be altered at all, and making changes where it *is* possible can have a prohibitive price tag.

The next things to consider—and if you're sensible, you'll think them through before you start your garden —are ergonomic efficiency and traffic patterns. Where are you going to situate the practical necessities, things such as garbage cans, clotheslines, compost bins, firewood, hoses and garden tools? If you have kids, where are they going to play? Do they need or want a sandbox, swing set or pool? For all of these, you will need to think about convenience, security and aesthetics, which—as you will find—rarely blend together gracefully.

Your next task will be to think carefully and realistically about who you are and how you live. If you're an animal-loving, child-rearing, ecology-minded person with a demanding occupation, that will dictate what you ought to do with your compact garden: things will have to be sturdy, fences will be necessary and recycling areas extensive. If you're a busy urban professional

□ □ □ □ □

PROBLEM SOLVING

Landscaping in a compact garden is an entirely different ballgame than in a larger garden. In a larger garden, landscaping is usually intended to create a specific effect. In a restricted space, it is more often called upon to solve particular problems. I have a friend who owns a very long, skinny two-storey house covered with white vinyl siding. Her lot slopes down to the end of her property abruptly enough to give her vertigo when she stands on the wide deck that spans the back of the house.

The space beneath the deck has proved to be very useful: she keeps her composter and wheelbarrow there, along with whatever yard debris she hasn't found a home for. The drawback is that when she stands at the bottom of her garden and looks back (perhaps doing the one-eye exercise described on page 13), it is not an appealing sight. My first suggestion was that she stay away from the bottom of her garden, but that was unproductive advice. We hit upon the idea of creating a shrub bed at the base of the deck, a piece of landscaping that would accomplish two tasks: it would conceal the underdeck's storage area, and it would visually ease the abrupt rise of the deck from the yard.

who lives alone, travels regularly on business and likes to go sailing on weekends, it won't do your sanity any good to set up a garden that demands a lot of time and energy. If you're a homebody with ambitions as an amateur plant geneticist and a love of privacy, that will dictate its own set of gardening options. There can be as many different kinds of gardens as there are people to enjoy them. The trick is to enjoy them, rather than be driven wild by the demands they make or by the guilt that ensues when you are unable to meet those demands.

But no matter who you are or what your interests, you owe it to yourself and to the gods and goddesses of gardening to do what I call the one-eye exercise. Go out into your yard, close one eye and squint. Ask yourself what you see that you like and what you see that you don't like. Then take a longer squinting look, and imagine the best possible garden you are capable of dreaming up. Repeat the exercise several times a year – at least once in midsummer and once in the dead of winter.

When you've done all these things, it is time to start thinking more practically. Make a plan of that dream garden. Try to determine how much time

and energy you will have for gardening, add 50 percent to both (because gardening always takes more time and resources than you expect), and start making some choices.

The first choices are basic ones. For instance, if your main goal is to create shade, privacy and pleasant landscaping, you are probably going to have a difficult time growing sun-loving flowers and vegetables. If you want to garden for seasonal floral displays or vegetable production, you would do well to keep heavy-rooting, shade-producing plants out of your garden. No amount of money or cunning will make tomatoes compatible with large shade trees.

If you are really stubborn, you can try to have everything you want. Many beginners valiantly attempt to do just that, until experience teaches them different. There are ways to achieve a reasonable compromise, but your plantings will have to be carefully made and intelligently laid out to take advantage of the assets of your space. And someone is going to have to put in some hard labour to make it come out right.

□   USING WHAT YOU HAVE

When facing any long-term project, it's a good idea to start by taking stock of

On sunny days, the stone wall bordering this driveway will act as a heat sink for the plants growing at its base. The creation of this garden transformed a long, narrow, sunny space into a beautiful spot while simultaneously distracting attention from the functional woodshed at the end of the drive.

what you have and—sometimes more important—what you don't have.

□ *Light*

One of the most important initial calculations you will have to make for a compact garden concerns sunlight—how much your garden gets, which direction it comes from and how to use it most productively. If your back garden faces south, consider yourself lucky: you will be able to take advantage of full sunlight for most of the day, and it happens that the majority of plants prefer direct sunlight. If your garden faces north, you have a problem because your building and the ones around it are likely to block out a great deal of the incoming light. Shade-loving plants are not as plentiful as sun lovers, and they are often more difficult to cultivate. If you have a shady garden and you are really determined to grow

tomatoes, you'll have to consider removing some of the obstructions—such as trees—and you'll definitely have to become creative about where you place your tomato beds. (In an extreme case, you might even have to think about moving.) If your space faces east or west, your gardening prospects lie somewhere in between, depending on building heights and the other characteristics of the streetscape.

When I bought my present house, one of the most important considerations in my decision to purchase was that the garden faced south. That allowed me to scale my plantings to take advantage of the full days of sunlight coming into the yard. I've kept large vines and tree plantings close to the house so that they don't block light to the garden. The house is an older one, built at the turn of the century, and it is quite tall. Consequently, the small

This all-green garden emphasizes foliage rather than flowers. The broad curled hosta leaves are set off by the spears of iris and echoed by the day lilies at the rear. The waterfall and pool bordered by ground-creeping evergreens and textured deciduous foliage create a real sense of a private, peaceful woodland spot.

front lot is almost always in shade. I've planted trees there, ones that I thought could handle shade until they eventually grow tall enough to take care of their own light requirements. One of them, a snowball tree, turned out to be a bad choice, and it soon died. These things happen. Because shade-loving annuals are a little more common and less demanding than shade-loving perennials and larger permanent plant species, I use annuals extensively in shady areas.

□   *Water Table and Hydrology*

An important consideration in small-lot gardening and one that is frequently ignored, the water table is governed by local topography and soil type as much as by annual and seasonal levels of sunshine and rain. In my neighbourhood, the soils are quite dense and clayey and the water table in winter is relatively high because the main part of the area is at the bottom of a gradual slope. Before the city was settled, a small creek probably ran right through my yard.

The natural hydrology—the way water moves in a given area—has been radically altered in most settled city neighbourhoods, and these alterations can pose problems for gardeners. It's a good idea to figure out what would be occurring in your neighbourhood if nature had been left to itself, because to some extent, nature tries to pursue its original course. Occasionally it succeeds in strange ways, and there are times when it is worth our while to keep things unnatural. The most common tactic for low-lying areas is to raise the level of a garden by adding topsoil, but drainage systems—which have different ranges of efficiency and cost—are another option. They can also be fun to experiment with.

Other neighbourhoods in this city, many of them not far from here, have excellent hydrology and completely different subsoil conditions created by landform events thousands and even millions of years ago. There, the advantages and disadvantages are completely different. Winter root soaking is no problem, but because water drains so well, it is often difficult to maintain proper moisture levels during the hot summer months. Similarly, lime and fertilizers tend to leach out more quickly. More care must be taken in applying them, or their effects will be disappointingly temporary. Your own city or town will probably have an equal degree of variety in soil and water-table conditions. They are good things to know about.

□   *Soil*

Generally, the smaller a gardening lot is, the better the soil needs to be. Soil is extremely important, and later, I'll be devoting a section to evaluating your soil, building it up and keeping it productive (see pages 30-33).

□   CLIMATE AND CLIMATIC ZONES

I live in Vancouver, British Columbia, where the climate is relatively mild. The gardening parameters here are generous, adventurous gardening is the rule, and minor gardening disasters, as a consequence, are frequent. British Columbia is supposed to be a paradise for gardeners, but it is also a paradise for fungi and slugs. The summers aren't hot, which causes difficulties with heat-loving plants, and the winters are more often rainy and damp than cold and icy. Still, we get enough snow and frost to make our winters more similar, from a gardener's point of view, to a Denver or Toronto winter than to one in California, where there are no rules at all.

Climate ought to be understood in three ways: there are macroclimates, mesoclimates and microclimates (also known as large, medium and small climates), and each affects what you can do as a gardener. As a quick rule of thumb, let's say that for Canadian and U.S. gardeners, two basic macroclimates exist: California and non-California. By California, I mean southern California, parts of the southern United States and Florida—anyplace where winter doesn't have regular and profound biotic consequences. Non-California regions experience a season, with widely varying degrees of severity, during which plants become dormant and tender varieties can die if temperatures drop too low.

This book is basically intended for gardeners who have to contend with unavoidable winter frosts and who live north of the California macroclimate, and so its general techniques and their applications can be used across most of North America.

It would be nice if it were simply a question of macroclimates, but it isn't. Within each of these is a series of mesoclimatic zones that need to be taken into account. The plants you can grow in Toronto or Cleveland are very different from those that can be grown in St. John's, Newfoundland, or Portland, Oregon. Along the West Coast, for instance, you will generally have at your disposal the same range of gardening options that British gardeners do—too many to count, in other words. Across the Canadian Prairies and the midwestern United States, the winters are more severe and unpredictable, so choices will be limited to hardier varieties. In southern Ontario and Quebec as well as in the Great Lakes area of the United States and the northeastern seaboard, the winters sometimes make you feel as if you're living in Labrador or Greenland, but the hot, humid summers that follow open up all kinds of gardening possibilities, particularly with annual plants. (Success with tender perennials is often governed less by climatic limitations than by how much trouble you're willing to take to protect the plants from the elements.) In other words, each area has its assets and its drawbacks.

Average minimum winter temperature, the frost-free period and annual rainfall are important parameters, but

they can be compensated for to some degree with a combination of technology and plain, old-fashioned hard work. If you're prepared to spend the time and money (and to expose yourself to occasional ridicule by your friends and neighbours), you can do amazing or absurd things with plants. There are people here in Vancouver, for instance, who have palm trees in their gardens. The truth is that it is far too cold for palm trees here, and in frigid weather, their owners have been known to wrap them with blankets or to erect the silliest and most expensive heating contraptions imaginable. People who are willing to spend three days outside in a blizzard hugging a palm tree that ought to be a thousand miles to the south are obviously crazy. They are also wonderful, and if 30 or 40 percent of the population instead of 0.01 percent were like them, our cities would be much safer, more interesting and more beautiful places to live in.

If you want to indulge these kinds of interests, you have to be prepared to live the way farmers do: you've got to spend an awful lot of time in the garden, and you've got to be willing to be there whenever a climate-based emergency hits. If you want your activities to be a little more diversified, you need to be sensible.

Macro- and mesoclimates are one consideration, but microclimates are quite another, and I think their impact is something that is often seriously underrated. Microclimates—or neighbourhood climates—are frequently as important as the theoretical climatic description of a city or region. Within most cities and regions, there occurs a wide variety of distinct microclimates. They are dictated by elevation, by proximity to heat or light and by obstructing objects and landforms. They are affected by bodies of water, by the direction, velocity and frequency of wind, by soil type and by hydrology and water-table behaviour.

After decades of gardening in differ-

NO SPRINKLERS

Watering gardens is one of the practices most people take for granted. But while all plants require water, they don't all want it in the same way or in the same quantities. The risk of diminishing productivity, both floral and vegetable, by inept watering is quite real. Water from a sprinkler, for instance, isn't like rainwater. It is considerably colder, because it hasn't had time to reach air temperature, and the quantities are often excessive.

Most cities have bylaws to control garden watering. Aside from conserving public water supplies, these guidelines and restrictions—if they don't prohibit watering altogether—can actually help your garden. Most confine garden watering to alternate days or prohibit the use of sprinklers during the daylight hours. Luckily, healthy gardens don't need daily sprinkling, and they don't ever need it in the middle of the day. I recommend morning showers both for human beings and for gardens. Watering your garden in the evening is better than doing it at midday, but a wise gardener will remember that nighttime waterings often fill the swimming pool for slugs and other pests, all of whom love an evening dip.

ent microclimates, I've concluded that urban and suburban gardeners should pay much more attention to these highly specific local considerations than they do. Take a look around, talk to your neighbours, and find out what they know. Pay attention to what you learn. What works in your neighbourhood is often not going to work just a mile away, and what can be done in your garden is often not possible three or four doors away.

The climatic-zone map on page 121 will give you an indication of the zone in which you live. Consult this map, and talk to the experts at local garden centres to get an idea of the environmental particulars of your area before you decide what you will try to grow in your garden.

GARDENING WITH THE NEIGHBOURS

□

Layered shrubs and trees have been used to break what might otherwise have been a bleak, dark view to the street between two downtown buildings. Geraniums and pansies in window boxes and containers have been added for colour, while the lower branches of the trees have been pruned away to provide a feeling of openness.

Living and gardening in cities have their challenges, and some of them will test your interpersonal skills more than your gardening skills. The smaller your lot, the more your garden will be affected by what your neighbours have done, are doing and will do. And that is something you will have to come to terms with right at the beginning.

When I moved into my house, the lot was filled with trees, all of them dead. In conversation with my other neighbours, I learned that my then next-door neighbour — clearly an overmeticulous ratepayer — had garrotted each of my trees with wire the previous year because he didn't like leaves falling onto his immaculately clipped lawn. I had some rather choice words with him af-

ter I found out what he'd done to my trees. The fact that I'm not quite the passive person my predecessor obviously was may have influenced my neighbour's subsequent decision to sell, particularly after I dumped one of the stumps over the fence onto his beloved lawn. When he rushed out to complain, I told him that he could dispose of the stump however he liked, since he'd killed the tree. When he threatened to call the police, I announced that I was a city planner and that I had documented evidence that he'd killed my trees. If he wanted to complain to the authorities, I went on, he'd find himself in even more hot water than he was already. I was bluffing, of course, but the bluff succeeded. He didn't make the phone call, and a few weeks later, he put up a For Sale sign.

I don't want to give the impression that I do this sort of thing often or that I'm surrounded by evil neighbours. I'm only a monster when provoked. That man was the only truly bad neighbour I've run into, and he's now long gone. I'm tempted to say "and forgotten," but the enthusiasm with which I have just recounted the story would make the claim absurd.

Peaceably negotiating the human element is one thing. The physical challenge a neighbouring yard can present is something else again. It is vital to think carefully about the placement of trees, garages and fences in adjacent yards when you're planning your own garden. An adjoining yard that is heavily treed, for instance, makes for real difficulties if you're trying to grow plants that require full sun. In a south-facing garden, a neighbour's garage right against the property line can block light and restrict air movement over part of your property, creating a cool spot for part of the day. In a different configuration, it might create a hot spot that you can take advantage of. Similarly, a bordering cedar hedge not only blocks light but puts down roots that make planting near it problematic.

In fact, even if your neighbours have grassed over or paved their entire lot, it is going to affect you. People who like grass usually dislike having coarse weeds poking through their carpet of green. To get rid of them, they'll often use herbicides that can spill onto or drain across to your soil. If one of your neighbours is the sort who lays concrete or asphalt across the backyard and parks the car there, such toxic substances as oil and gas may find their way into your yard.

Even if your neighbour is an avid gardener, what he or she plants may not be compatible with what you have in mind. Whatever is going on next door, your neighbour is going to have a much greater effect on your garden than if you lived on several acres outside of town. Usually problems can be worked out easily with a conversation across the fence. They are worth attending to, but don't be surprised if they sometimes turn out to be a little unsettling.

Don't get depressed. It isn't impossible to garden this way. In fact, it makes it more interesting. Having neighbours close to you is an asset that can make for some enjoyment.

☐ *SOME ADVANTAGES OF CRAMPED QUARTERS*

I live in a neighbourhood that is culturally very mixed. On the lot to the west lives a Chinese family, part of an extended family whose other members live right across the alley. Next door on the east side is a Chilean family — not passionate gardeners, but terrific cooks. Next to them are Archie and Phyllis, who come from around here. They are the most meticulous gardeners I've ever met in my life. They have lived in their house for nearly 40 years and are the unofficial historians in the neighbourhood. Beyond them are several Portuguese families. Across the alley and down the street a little way lives Karla, who is, I think, from one of the Balkan countries. There are several more Chinese families on the block, as well as a couple of East Indian families.

Most of us don't have a great deal in common, occupationally or culturally. The Chinese family, for instance, is very close and insular, and the two sets of grandparents barely speak English. The Portuguese families tend to stick together, particularly during wine-making season, when they get fairly noisy about sticking together. There is, however, one thing we all have in common: we're all gardeners. It's a rare day out in the garden when I don't talk to one or more of them about something. One of my regular weekend pleasures is to take a stroll down the alley to check on what they and their gardens are up to. Almost everyone else does the same.

It's more than merely a pleasant thing

HOUSE CALLS

If you've just moved in and want to meet a few of your new neighbours, you don't have to throw a big party and invite them over for drinks. On the first pleasant morning, take a shovel, go out into your new garden and dig a hole. I can say with some authority that within minutes they will start to appear.

I learned this by accident about a week after I moved into my present house. I had brought a small tree from my previous residence, and although spring had barely arrived, I decided to set it out in the garden. I met four of my neighbours within the first half hour, and I'm pretty sure they didn't just happen by. They gave me, one by one, their private history of my house and what had happened there before I arrived. Each tale, of course, was completely different. A week or two later, when I began the complicated task of removing a huge stump the previous owner had left for me, I could have sold tickets.

Try to dig your hole near the front sidewalk or close to the back of the property so that you and your new neighbours don't have to holler to be heard. Bringing out a few lawn chairs so that they can sit while they chat is a considerate touch.

to do. I've learned a great deal about gardening from talking over the fence with my neighbours—and more than a few things about life in general. One or two of my neighbours, I suspect, may even have learned from my techniques. The exchanges have taught me the most important secret of small-lot gardening: to respect and make use of the very real gardening expertise that exists around me.

All gardeners have certain plants they especially like to grow, and gardeners from different cultural backgrounds grow different kinds of plants, often by traditional methods they have adapted to local conditions. My Chinese neighbours, for instance, are superb vegetable gardeners, particularly when it comes to harvesting huge crops from a very limited space. Each year, they take three crops of bok choy from a small sunny patch next to my fence. As the summer heat comes on, they take advantage of my corn and bean crops to provide their bok choy with a little protection. And last summer, from a six- or eight-foot-long patch of carefully prepared soil, they grew an astounding number of huge exotic squashes and melons that sent vines sprawling right across their yard—and melons aren't supposed to grow well in this climate. I watch these neighbours like a hawk and have taken to using some of their methods.

A number of years ago, Karla gave me several varieties of pole beans I'd never seen before and have yet to find in any seed catalogue. In return, I gave her my extra 'Blue Lake' bean seeds. I liked these exotic pole beans so much that last year, I didn't even plant 'Blue Lake' beans. Instead, I turned them all over to Karla. She planted them very late in the season and, by wrapping the vines in plastic, was able to harvest fresh beans as late as early October.

The Portuguese families all grow wine grapes, something that the local garden centres warn not to expect too much from in this climate. But in our back al-

ley, their grape harvests are enormous, because they have a special way of getting around the shortage of summer heat: they grow the grapes across their garage roofs. Each garage has black asphalt shingles on the roof, and the grapevines, sitting about six to nine inches above it on special frames, absorb the reflected and retained heat.

I've gotten tips about the advantages of watering with warmed water and manure tea from my Chinese neighbours. Come to think of it, I could provide an example of something particular and unusual that each one of my neighbours does. Your own neighbourhood likewise will have experts and expertise simply waiting to be tapped. Sometimes the advice will come from the old-timers who have discovered by trial and error over the years what will grow well in the local soil and microclimate. If you're lucky enough to live in a culturally mixed neighbourhood, that's another resource. The advice you get from along the back alley and around the neighbourhood is likely to be as reliable as any you'll get from your local garden shop.

There is also a more tasty and tangible bonus when you have neighbours who garden—the wonderful opportunities for trading excess vegetables and flowers. I habitually grow more tomatoes than I need and can cleverly press my advantage, as they are usually earlier than my neighbours'. In return, I get bok choy from my Chinese neighbours, bedding plants and cut flowers from Archie and Phyllis and fresh dill from outside the fence of one of my Portuguese neighbours. He has more than he needs, and he has figured out a way to keep it coming from early July into October—lots of it. When I plant dill, it's all ready at the same time.

Another source of valuable information is the staff at the local garden centre. The problem is that much of the time, you'll end up talking to a concave teenager who would rather be surfing and who is probably wonder-

ing why you're trying to speak Latin to him. I suppose this has more to do with the current state of retail merchandising than anything else, but it can be irritating when it happens. In a lot of cases, it is a simple question of management being too stingy and shortsighted to realize that in a service industry—whether selling designer clothes, bicycles or gardening supplies—the staff should be informed about and interested in the products sold. One of the ways to get good, knowledgeable staff is to train them properly and then pay them well enough that they'll stick around. Then, when we ask questions in a garden shop, we would get informative answers instead of "Well, I dunno, I think you just plant it in the ground, sort of, like, and it's okay."

All this is a roundabout way of saying, "Don't believe everything you hear at the garden centre." If a clerk answers

a question with extremely specific instructions or goes off and finds someone who does know the answers, you've hit the jackpot. Knowledgeable gardeners do exist in these establishments, but you sometimes have to be fairly aggressive to find them. When you do find one, make that person an honorary part of your gardening neighbourhood.

◻ GOOD FENCES AND GOOD NEIGHBOURS

First of all, a philosophical question: Do good fences make good neighbours? American poet Robert Frost thought so, but the fences he had in mind—those made of thick stone—don't really do the trick in small-lot neighbourhoods. Yet the principle behind those stone fences does make sense. It's just that Mr. Frost was so busy propagandizing isolationism, he didn't see what his fence was meant to accomplish.

The author's backyard, featuring his beloved wisteria and his fence of choice—chain link. The lettuce is coming on strong, while the homemade cloche at right is carefully angled to release collected heat.

GARDEN BARBARIANS

Theft is one thing. Vandalism is another. I don't know whether there's more of it now than there used to be. There seems to be, but maybe I'm just getting older. God knows, I did my share of garden raiding when I was a kid, and I'm sure I was cursed in absentia as vigorously as today's raiders are. Occasionally, I've seen gardens that have been deliberately ravaged by vandals whose motives completely elude me. There are reasons to vandalize an ostentatious automobile— or so I'm told. But I can think of no reason in the world to destroy a beautiful garden, and it makes my heart sick when it happens. Most city dwellers are the victims of vandalism from time to time, and if there's any consolation to be taken, it lies in the fact that gardeners don't seem to be victimized any more than anyone else. In fact, gardeners may be victimized a little less often.

Those fences were conceived in Europe centuries ago as repositories for the stones farmers removed from their fields. They were only secondarily intended to divide property and people — agricultural devices rather than political or social institutions.

Fences are necessary between most small lots, but they should be built for the same kinds of reasons as Frost's misunderstood stone fences — to help gardeners, not to separate people. In light of that, you might deduce that I'm a fan of chain-link fencing. You're right. Chain-link fencing lets light through and allows air to move into and through the garden, both of which are important to garden health and success. If you want outdoor privacy, grow vines on your fence. When the cold weather arrives, you can cut the wind and protect delicate vines by tarping them.

If your fences are high enough (six or seven feet is the maximum allowable height in most cities), they can become invaluable garden resources for vegetable crops such as pole beans and tall peas and for a variety of trailing cucumbers and squashes. They are also useful for sweet peas, permanent vines and espaliered fruit trees.

Chain-link fencing doesn't have to be the prison-yard variety either. It is now available in a number of attractive vinyl-clad colours, and nobody ever said you couldn't paint the pipes. Special paints are required, but these, like the coloured vinyl, are readily obtainable. When I put up my fencing, I took things one step further, using standard three-inch heavy steel pipe and a British system of connectors called Kee Klamps that can be purchased from scaffolding companies. The initial material cost was greater than if I had bought the lighter, more common galvanized stuff available at lumber stores, but I was able to cut costs by installing it myself. I painted the pipes bright blue, and I haven't had a single complaint from my neighbours.

If you're stuck on wooden fencing, try to resist the solid-fence syndrome. I know solid fences are attractive and that they will make a yard very secluded. But they block light and air and afford thieves and vandals the opportunity to pillage your house and garden in privacy. So unless you're home all the time, I don't recommend them. Everyone wants to know what goes on inside a closed fence, and sooner or later, the wrong kind of curiosity may make you regret having installed it.

□　　　COMMON PROBLEMS

In case I've made neighbourhood gardening sound completely wonderful and easy, I must acknowledge that there are, in fact, some very real problems with it. Most, but not all of them, are people problems.

One thing you have to put up with is theft. I don't mean my occasional trips down the alley for a little dill or a passing stranger's sampling a few peas or beans that have grown over the fence. I've had potted plants stolen, and I've learned not to put certain crops — such as corn and tomatoes — near the fence. My neighbour Karla lost most of her tomatoes for three years running until she finally put up her own seven-foot chain-link fence. Last year, I lost some of my corn because I don't always get around to locking my gate.

I have two conflicting responses to garden thieves. The first is a sense that people who steal food need it or, at the very least, that they will enjoy it as much as I would. The second response is considerably less liberal, and I'll leave it to you to imagine what I'd like to do to any thief I caught in my garden.

Cats and sometimes dogs are another problem for neighbourhood gardeners. Because there are more houses — and therefore more families — in high-density neighbourhoods, there are more pets. That means fewer spots for the cats to dig in and less space for dogs to go adventuring in. It isn't as bad a problem in our neighbourhood as in some. Everybody gardens, so the damage done by pets is spread around fairly evenly. In any case, I really can't complain, because I have a cat and a large dog of my own.

Where I live – in a city of more than a million people – the real problem is with raccoons, one of several species of scavengers successfully adapting to urban living. Raccoons are cute, but they can do an incredible amount of damage in a garden. If you happen to see one, don't be friendly, and don't feed it. If you do, it will pay a return visit some night when you're not at home, bringing along its children, its boyfriend, its brothers, sisters, aunts or uncles. Usually they all come, and you won't have much of a garden left when they leave. If you have cats, the raccoons may harm them too.

In other areas, you may face coyotes or a variety of distant relatives of Mickey and Minnie Mouse. My advice is to live with the problems they create, but don't go out of your way to make friends. We'd be in a lot more trouble if these animals wouldn't – or couldn't – survive among us.

Finally, cities are catchalls for plant pests and diseases. The reasons are simple: more species of plants have been imported into our cities than anywhere else, and each has brought its own special pests and diseases with it. When soil and other organic materials are brought into cities, they, too, come with their own pests, weeds and diseases. Not surprisingly, the smaller the lot size in a neighbourhood, the greater these problems tend to be. They are not, however, insurmountable.

☐ *SOME SENSIBLE REMEDIES*

Remedies for some of the built-in problems of restricted-space gardening exist. You can help prevent theft and vandalism by setting up, formally or informally, a neighbourhood watch. Such organizations aren't perfect, but when they are in place, thieves soon seem to get the idea. The seven-foot pipe-and-mesh fence bordering my back alley

helps keep thieves and vandals out, even though I rarely lock the gate. Backyard lighting will help, especially if you use automatic switches that turn the lights on and off intermittently whether you're home or not.

Some people put Beware of Dog signs on their back gates even when they don't have a dog. One of my neighbours has such a sign, but she has dogs – two miniature terrier-poodle crosses. Both are at least 15 years old, stone-deaf and more or less blind. If they could see or hear an intruder, they wouldn't be able to catch him or her – they'd have trouble outrunning an earthworm. If they were lucky enough to catch or corner one by accident, they wouldn't be able to bite because they don't have any teeth. Once in a while, one of these dogs will blunder into my yard or someone else's – on occasion, I've found one standing in the street. When I notice one on that kind of adventure, I pick it up and let it gum my wrist while I drop it back inside its own yard.

On the whole, dogs are remarkably sensible beasts. If you aren't friendly, they don't come around much. Try barking at them when you see them. Dogs are terrified of rabid or otherwise crazy human beings, and besides, you might amuse your neighbours. If you keep a dog of your own, train it *never* to go in the garden.

Dogs are far more eager to please than most human beings are, and they quickly get the hang of "never" if you're emphatic enough about it. When my part-wolfhound was a pup, she buried just one bone in my onion patch. We had a fairly lengthy consciousness-raising seminar about why this was not acceptable, and she hasn't set foot in the garden since. That was four years ago. I hate to say it, but if you own a dog and can't get through to it about something like this, it's unlikely you'll have it long anyway. Untrained dogs don't survive in cities.

Cats are a mixed blessing for gardeners. On the downside, they scare away

TWILIGHT ZONING

In most cities, zoning regulations dictate that all houses must be built the same distance from the street regardless of the direction they happen to face. The setback can be 30 feet, and it is often quite a bit more. It isn't so important on streets that run north-south, but where they run east-west, people who live on the north side of the street lose a large proportion of their backyard sun space. It is particularly irritating and wasteful if you want to grow sun-loving plants.

What should have been instituted years ago when those regulations were devised is a zoning system in which north-side houses are set considerably closer to the street in order to allow more sunlight into their backyards.

Do you know the reason behind the standard setback? It's so the street looks symmetrical to anyone driving down it. Silly, eh? I've seen a few neighbourhoods built before standard setback regulations were instituted. Invariably, they have much more dynamic and interesting streetscapes as well as better gardening opportunities. But the apparent lack of visual order offends the jerks down at City Hall.

Not a casualty of the "setback" bylaw

on the books in so many municipalities,

this front yard can take advantage of full

sun. Because the house sits high on

the property, its owners have planted

tall shrubs around the steps to moderate

the rise. To the left of the sidewalk

is a colourful mix of sun-loving, self-

seeding annuals and perennials, and

to the right are roses underplanted with

dozens of bright poppies.

birds—an important component of nature's pest-control program. I have to put netting over the garden in the early spring and summer to prevent my cat and the neighbour's from digging up fragile new plantings. But cats do keep rodents away from both house and garden, and if they have an open and sandy patch to dig in, they may steer clear of established beds. I keep a small, shady patch of ground under the eaves of the house clear for my cat, which, being a cat, it perversely ignores. A lot of gardeners I know become psychotic when cats are mentioned, but I happen to admire them, partly because they are totally unaware that they are supposed to respect human beings, and partly because they love sunlight almost as much as plants do. Having cats around the garden is one of those invaluable reminders that life is meant to be pleasurable rather than perfect.

Whatever you do, don't bother investing in those silly dog- and cat-repellent sprays. They don't work at all, although they do manage to stink up the garden. One last note: having animals around should make you more careful about using pesticides.

FIRST STEPS: STARTING A GARDEN

□

If you don't know much about gardening, this section will be one that you'll find yourself rereading. It will be helpful whether you're starting a garden from scratch on a newly settled piece of ground or rebuilding a decayed garden in an established lot.

If you're going to have any kind of garden at all, there's a preliminary bit of advice you really should take: You'll need to make a plan. You don't have to stick to it, and to tell the truth, I recommend that you don't. But you should have some idea of what you want your garden to be, and you've got to make plans. And make plans. And make plans.

□ *MAKING A BASIC PLAN*

Remember, you're gardening in a neighbourhood and in relatively cramped quarters, so you have to take into account many more things than you might imagine—and some that will occur to you as you go along. And you will need to make choices. Make an inventory of assets and liabilities.

Which direction does your chosen garden area face? How much light do

23

you get? What hours of the day do you get it? Which are the brightest spots? What special problems do you have, such as light-blocking trees or adjacent buildings? Are there any significant eyesores you want your landscaping to block out (like a messy neighbouring yard or that hot pink bungalow with bright yellow trim just across the alley)? Finally, how much time and energy do you have, what kind of physical condition are you in, and how long are you prepared to have your yard looking like a war zone? About these last questions, be practical and be honest with yourself. I've seen gardeners start ambitious projects they couldn't support with either funds or effort, and the result is usually no garden at all or a lot of anxiety, often both. If you're not rich or if you're strapped for time, break your ambitious plans down into small projects you can tackle one at a time.

One of the best ideas I've come across is that of keeping a garden journal. Buy a looseleaf binder, and divide it into sections. Here are some suggestions about how to organize your journal.

□   *Master Plan*

You need a master plan, even if you don't stick to it. Make this the first sec-

tion of your garden journal. It should contain your inventory of assets and liabilities and at least a few of your dreams, however silly they might seem later. It will help you to work out your priorities and to identify problem areas. Most of all, it will keep you from standing in your garden with a shovel in your hand, a dazed look on your face and alligators all around as you try to remember just what it was you set out to accomplish. Without a plan, you can waste enormous amounts of time and startling amounts of cash when one project collides with or supersedes a previous venture.

□   *Maps*

Draw a map of your garden. Each time you change it, add another map. It will help you keep track of what you've planned and of how your ideas changed as you learned more. I also keep an annual annotated map of my vegetable plantings to help plan crop rotations. It also serves as a record of which plants grew well in which locations. (There have been some surprises—plants don't always do what they're supposed to do—and it's important to keep track of them.) A map of bulb plantings is also a must, because bulbs die back in the

With raised beds made of railway ties and established trees in the neighbouring garden providing dappled shade, this stripped-down yard is a garden waiting to happen.

24

Before and after: a couple of months later, the garden shown at left is now in full swing, complete with a sitting area at the rear. The plants in need of extra drainage have been placed on the second level, while the tougher drought-resistant varieties are down in front.

summer and it can be difficult to recall exactly where they are when later plants grow up around them. A bulb map is also useful when you're planting more for the following spring. Augmenting your sketches with photographs taken throughout the growing season is a valuable exercise as well.

☐ *A Timetable of Planting Dates*

Keep a record of your planting dates for different things. I suggest you divide your schedule into two sections: one for annuals and one for perennials. The timetable will help you determine your microclimate from month to month and year to year.

☐ *Bright Ideas*

I keep a section for all the wonderful ideas I get about what to plant and where to plant it, along with notes on things to try in the coming season.

Most of the ideas turn out to be loony, but even they make for amusing reading in the winter or succeeding years.

I also keep a record of my disasters, noting what happened and when, why I think it happened and how I can avoid it the next time. This section has quite a few pages, as you've no doubt already figured out.

☐ *BASIC GARDENING TOOLS*

Gardening demands two things: time and a reasonably strong back. As with most activities, however, it is almost impossible to avoid the accumulation of more tangible items, the few tools you can't garden without. You'll need at least the following:

☐ *Primary Tools*

☐ A shovel, preferably long-handled, because of the increased leverage a long handle provides. I keep a selection of shovels around, including a short-handled, half-sized one for delicate jobs. Even the best shovels get old, and the handles break.

□ A spade – again, preferably long-handled, to use for edging and lifting sod. As far as I can see, the only advantage of short-handled shovels is that you can hang them with the blade pointing downward.

□ A spading fork, short-handled. Here, the short handle makes sense, because forks are characteristically used to lift and turn soil and compost. The tines on a cheap fork bend very easily, which makes the tool useless.

□ A strong metal standard garden rake. If your garden is very small, buy a half-sized version.

□ A mallet. I use this to pound stakes into the ground. The head on an ordinary hammer will split most stakes.

□ Good hand clippers and pruning shears. Hand clippers must be kept oiled and away from the elements.

□ Some plastic buckets: at least a one-gallon and a five-gallon and an ordinary garbage can.

□   *Secondary (or Shared) Tools*

□ A lawn mower.

□ A wheelbarrow.

□ An assortment of hand trowels and cultivators and perhaps a fan rake.

□ A hose, a hand nozzle and a watering wand with a mesh nozzle.

□ A piece of quarter-inch metal screen in a solid two-by-three-foot frame.

A warning: Don't buy cheap tools. They are made of cheap materials, and they'll wear out or break before you know it and probably at exactly the wrong time. If you do buy cheap tools, you'll invariably wind up going back to the garden shop or hardware store for better ones, usually right when you want to be in the garden.

Garden tools come in three grades: bargain-basement, serviceable and designer. The cheapest variety is usually on sale, is brightly coloured and has about a three-hour guarantee (redeem-

able only by presenting the defective tool in person to the manufacturer, undoubtedly located somewhere in Southeast Asia or eastern Europe).

Serviceable tools are generally made in North America, are not brightly coloured and are never on sale. If you want to own designer tools, you can find them in some seed catalogues and in bric-a-brac boutiques. If you're after the absolute best, get hold of the Lee Valley Tools catalogue (see Sources). Their products are the Cadillacs of gardening tools, and some of them will make you drool. Designer hand tools aren't generally a sensible buy, but you can sometimes acquire them by putting them on your Christmas list. If someone bought me a real live Lee Valley shovel, I think I'd keep it on the mantel. It would be just too beautiful to get dirty.

An inexpensive way of obtaining quality garden tools is to cruise garage sales. The tools you get will be used, but if they were made right in the first place, that just gives them character. Garden tools were of better quality before the bargain-basement mentality conquered the world, so the older they are, the better, provided they have been well cared for. (Wipe the blades clean after use,

One of a gardener's best friends, a deep-bucketed wheelbarrow with an air-filled tire will stand you in good stead for years. Well balanced and able to take a reasonable load, it will come in handy for soil rebuilding, sod relocation or taking the kids for a spin.

MAKING LISTS

Some of the best tools you will use are the ideas you carry in your head or write down in your garden journal. When I was in the early "hard work" stages of my present garden, my ideas about what I wanted to accomplish often kept me working long after I had stopped feeling like it.

But the really important tools of this sort are straightforward inventory items. You need to have a clear idea of how deep your soil is and what basic qualities it has or doesn't have so that you can rebuild it as you go. You should also know a little about the prevailing wind direction, if there is one, because cold winter winds can kill exposed plants and chilly spring winds can set back growing plants or damage others that have fragile blossoms. I will provide a simple method of determining what your soil and water table are like, but these are the kinds of questions you should also learn, as a beginner, to ask your neighbours about. Conditions can change from yard to yard and block to block, and you'll be surprised at how much the old-timers know about local hydrology and soil.

and do it with an oiled cloth. Once a season, rub the wooden handles with mineral oil. Also, store your tools in a protected spot. I've never done any of this in my life, but I know I should.)

I've excluded from my list some common tools, such as cultivators and hoes. In a small garden, you should be planting crops closer together than you would on Rolling Acres, and you're better off on your hands and knees with smaller hand cultivators. Besides hoes and cultivators are a large number of what I call "gee-whiz" gadgets you can buy. Some of them work, others don't. Don't expect them to be as useful as advertised, and they won't be as useful as the tools I've listed above. Never buy a gee-whiz gadget from a catalogue; they never seem to work the way they're supposed to.

Buy a decent wheelbarrow, one with a fairly deep bucket and an air-filled tire. You'll use it a lot, particularly while building or rebuilding a garden. The cheaper ones are usually too shallow, and they tip over too easily. If you can swing it, it is worthwhile sharing one with a neighbour, because wheelbarrows take up quite a lot of storage space.

Since you aren't likely to have acres of grass, a good hand mower will probably do. I have an electric mower because I discovered that they work terrifically well in the fall for chopping up dead leaves and garden debris for the compost pile. On a small lot, the cord on an electric model really isn't much of an inconvenience. Don't buy a gas mower. They're noisy, and they can, and eventually will, pollute the soil. Weedeaters are useful devices if you've got a lot of corners in your garden. I use mine as frequently as I do the mower. Don't get one of the fancy ones with a gas-driven motor. As with other tools, don't buy a cheap one.

Spend a little money on your hoses. The cheap ones get kinks in them, and they burst easily under pressure. Any hose you can easily bend back to a 180-degree angle in the store is not

a good hose. I have a variety of different sprinklers, most of which I've picked up at garage sales, and I use them only for the lawn in the early spring before the garden comes up or when I'm feeling lazy. As important as hoses, incidentally, are water buckets. As I've said, flowering plants don't like sprinklers, because the unnaturally large water drops damage the petals. In the flower garden, I use a bucket or a watering wand so that I can provide water directly to the roots of each plant. Many garden plants, such as tomatoes and cucumbers, don't like abrupt temperature changes. The water that comes right from the hose or sprinkler is usually considerably colder than rainwater, and it can cause root shock. I use a plastic garbage can for these special waterings, filling it up in the evening so that the water is roughly at air temperature for morning waterings.

The framed quarter-inch metal screen may seem an odd tool, but I use mine constantly to filter heavy soil, to separate weeds from soil and to wash or sun-dry a variety of crops such as onions and garlic. The metal screen, which some people call hardware cloth, is available at most building-supply stores, and you can construct a simple frame using scrap 2-by-4s. Don't make it too heavy to move around easily, but it should be heavy enough to stand the weight of a shovelful of dirt tossed onto it from a distance.

□   *Rototillers*

You see and hear a lot about these machines, and the ads for them seem to say they are indispensable for the home gardener. They're made out to be great time and labour savers and excellent soil cultivators. I don't agree. For the small-lot gardener, they're inefficient, cumbersome and expensive, and they don't do even an adequate job of cultivating the soil. Give me a shovel and fork any day.

My real objection to rototillers is that they dig weeds and grasses back into the soil, a practice that isn't a great idea at the best of times and definitely isn't smart in a small garden. Weeds that have been turned under often grow back, and so will grasses, unless you're putting them at least a foot under the surface. No rototiller I've ever seen digs that deep. I use my screen rack to dry clumps of nonseeding grasses and broad-leafed weeds until they are dead. Then I compost them. If you just dump them on top of the compost heap while they have a breath of life left in them, they'll think it's Christmas.

BUILDING OR REBUILDING A GARDEN

People who have never gardened before generally have very strong ideas about what they'd like to achieve in their new gardens and how much effort and financial outlay it will take to produce the desired effect. Like most strongly held opinions, these usually include wildly underestimated notions of the cost of turning their dreams into reality. No matter what kind of garden you inherit—a gravel parking lot, a real but derelict garden or a tiny version of Versailles—the initial stages of gardening are time-consuming and quite costly. Before you bring out the wrecking ball, force yourself to be realistic about what you're up against. Changing an established garden can be as disruptive, arduous and expensive as starting from scratch.

Many beginning gardeners choose a house that already has a pretty garden. Although it is enticing to think of inheriting a beautiful garden, it isn't always a wise move. The better you get to know your lot and neighbourhood and the more particular your knowledge of gardening becomes, the more likely you are to be dissatisfied with a garden created by someone else. In many respects, it is easier to start from scratch or to rebuild a badly decayed garden than to renovate an established garden that is either inappropriate to your life style or not to your taste. One reason is that serious gardeners tend to put permanent structures—such as concrete beds and large trees—in their gardens. The other reason is that it is morally as well as physically difficult to remove perfectly healthy plant species simply because you dislike them.

An early warning: No matter what you start with, you *are* going to have to work pretty hard while you're rebuilding. Fortunately, that will also prove to be a big advantage. You will become intimate with the soil as you work, and that intimacy will serve you well in the long run. There are other advantages too, not the least of which is the sense of accomplishment you will experience from turning a derelict patch of ground into a productive and beautiful one. Sure, along the way, you'll get some exercise—quite a lot, actually. If you're not up to it, hire somebody to do the bull work. I recommend hiring a student. They don't complain much, and they don't mind being supervised. Pay them well too. They represent our future, and they'll work harder if they're well paid. (If you pay them really well, it might even save you the experience of seeing one of them stare at you blankly across the counter the next time you're at the garden centre.) Whatever you do, make sure the basics get done properly.

If it happens that there are unhealthy or dead trees on your property, my advice is to clear them out right away—and hire someone else to do it. I cleared six dead trees—several of them very large—from my lot by myself. It took most of one autumn, and I ended up with a very sore back and some permanent enemies down at the tool-rental agency where I acquired—and destroyed—several chain saws and come-alongs (cable-hoist devices for heavy lifting and pulling jobs). If I had it to do again, I would have it done by a professional. Clearing trees is very hard work

TREES UNDER SIEGE

These days, entire species of trees are becoming extinct or sick because of the massive amounts of pollutants humans are pumping into the environment. On the West Coast, for instance, both native and exotic dogwoods are in danger of dying out because of airborne pollutants, and a series of viruses is threatening to eradicate a number of willow species, including the weeping willow. (The rest of the tree species in the region are threatened by people with chain saws, but that is a political, not a gardening, problem.) In the east, acid rain is threatening a wide variety of trees, including the maples which make autumns in that part of the continent the most splendid on the planet. Over the last few decades, several species of trees have been wiped out by diseases, and several more are in danger of disappearing. The most spectacular and heartbreaking example is that of the elm, which has been destroyed by Dutch elm disease in all but isolated pockets of eastern North America. Unfortunately, about all a city gardener can do about it is to make sure tree roots get adequate supplements of lime, to join an environmental coalition and to try to toss bad governments out on their ears.

and requires expensive specialized tools (like chain saws and come-alongs) and a good deal of expertise. If you do hire professionals, make a point of lurking in the vicinity while they work. That way, not only can you see how they do what they do, but—and this is more important—you can insist that they remove as much of the roots as is humanly and technologically possible. Large decaying roots can affect hydrology over wide areas and may eventually sink beneath a sidewalk or permanent bed. They can cause considerable expense and aesthetic disruption years after you've forgotten they exist.

□ *HOW TO SPOT THE WRONG KIND OF TREE*

There are several "wrong" kinds of tree and many ways of detecting them. The three basic types are: the dead, the sick and the ugly. Here are some handy hints for determining which is which.

A deciduous tree is dead if it doesn't have leaves by midsummer; a coniferous tree is dead if the needles are bright orange or not present at all. Cut such trees down and remove the stumps pronto.

Sick trees present a far more complicated dilemma. The most beautiful species are often very fragile and may require specialized environments. If you have a sick tree on your property and you happen to like it, find out everything you can about it from reference books and local experts and decide whether it can be saved. If it is small enough and you have discovered that the problem is its location, you can move it to a better spot. (Do this in the late fall, winter or early spring while the tree is dormant, and recognize that the odds are against its survival no matter when you transplant.)

The difference between sick and ugly trees is often hard to distinguish. A tree may be ugly because you simply don't like its looks, but it can also be ugly because it is diseased. Really ugly trees do exist, although ugliness is generally a matter of the viewer's own perception.

For instance, I think most plantings of coniferous trees are unappealing in a small garden. They block light, and they tend to create acidic environmental conditions. If they are large enough, they make fine homes for raccoons and other pests. Yet other people think conifers are splendid. Who knows what goes on in the minds of such people? Maybe the trees remind them of Santa Claus.

If you have an ugly tree, be sure it is the tree itself that displeases you and not a disease. Sometimes all it needs is intelligent pruning and a disease-curing regimen. If your ugly tree is large, I recommend consulting a professional arborist before you take it out. Again, if it is large, have it done professionally.

□ *STARTING FROM SCRATCH*

Once you've cleared your garden space of dead, unhealthy and inappropriate trees, you'll probably have little more than tired-out, leached soil, a moss-filled, bumpy lawn and a whole lot of noxious weeds. Before you make another move, figure out roughly how much of the lot you want for your garden. You don't have to be precise about it, since you'll probably change your mind several times along the way. Before coming to any further decisions, you should do a couple of tests.

□ *The Hole Test*

The best way to proceed without hiring an engineering firm is to dig some holes. What you're trying to find out is fairly rudimentary stuff. You want to know how high your water table is and how quickly water is going to sift down to it. You also want to know how deep your topsoil is, where the subsoil is and what sits underneath. If, for instance, you find hardpan clay or rock a foot beneath the surface, water is going to sit on top. If you find gravel, your drainage is going to be swift and efficient. These things are important for both planting and summer watering.

Dig four or five holes in a variety of locations in your chosen garden space.

Make the holes as narrow as you can, and go down to a depth of two feet or until you hit the hard subsoil or run into gravel or rock. Don't fill the holes in right away. You'll need them for some further tests in the next few days.

If you're making your garden in an established city neighbourhood, chances are you will discover that you have anywhere from eight inches to two feet or more of topsoil. You can easily distinguish subsoil from topsoil because subsoils are usually lighter in colour and have more rock in them. Subsoil is also pretty well devoid of the nutrients and humus that plants need to grow well.

If you're conducting your tests in the fall or early spring, check to see whether your test hole fills with water. If water appears within 5 to 15 minutes and if it fills the hole more than a third full, you've got a high water table, which is both a problem and a blessing. Your garden will be slower to get going in the spring but will require less watering during the summer.

If you're testing during a dry period, drop the hose into the hole, fill it with water and watch what happens. If the hole empties fairly quickly — say, within five minutes — your soil is probably too light: there is not enough humus. If the hole takes much longer than five minutes to empty, your soil either is extremely heavy or has been compacted by years of people tromping across it. Usually, you will have both problems — in different parts of your garden — and they can be solved only by adding more humus and nutrients and by doing lots of digging.

□　　　　　*The Hand Test*

Take a handful of the topsoil you've dug out of the holes and examine it carefully. Ideal soil will have few or no rocks in it and will break apart easily if you squeeze it. Once squeezed, however, it should not sift away between your fingers, nor should it be too light or too heavy. In my experience, the colour of soil is not an indicator of quality. I've seen sandy-coloured soils that were superior to any black soil I've encountered. A good soil will just sit there in your hand, succulent and throbbing. Maybe a few earthworms will slither between your fingers and make a break for it. If your soil is like that, you're in luck. It's the gardener's equivalent of winning the lottery. Unfortunately, very few beginning gardeners win this lottery, and if you don't, you'll need to renovate your soil.

□　　*BUILDING YOUR TOPSOIL*

Once you have a rough idea of the assets and liabilities of your soil, water table and neighbourhood landscape, your first task is to improve the soil. If you feel the need to get scientific about it, you can either buy your own soil-testing kit or send a soil sample to the government agricultural agency in your area. In most locales, these agencies will do a basic analysis for a moderate fee. I don't think this is terribly accurate or useful for small gardens, most of which have endured so much tinkering on the part of all their previous owners that the soil varies considerably throughout the garden.

To create a decent bed, you will need at least 18 inches of good topsoil. Some organic gardeners like to have two feet, and a few books will say you need only 12 inches, but if you plan to garden in a small space, aim for at least 18 inches. You can make up a surprising amount of what you lack in horizontal space with generous soil depth.

If you haven't got 18 inches, you will have to obtain it, usually by buying a load or part load of topsoil. But before you do that, calculate how much you need. Suppliers deliver soil by the cubic yard, and most trucks carry at least 10 of those. Once you've calculated your requirements, add 25 percent to that figure. Soil — particularly good soil — will settle after it is delivered. If you figure you will need 5 cubic yards, buy 7. If you need 10, buy 13. The more you buy, the cheaper it gets.

□ □ □ □ □

CONTAINER SOIL

I don't have much use for the bagged soil that is often sold at supermarkets in the spring for outdoor planting, and most of the garden-shop outdoor soil isn't much better unless it is specially mixed in-house. Often what you get is nothing more than heavy peat soil mixed with half-rotted steer manure, and it is frequently too heavy, nitrogen-rich and acidic.

If your containers aren't large or numerous, you can probably afford to enjoy the better results you will get with sterilized indoor potting soils. If your containers are large and numerous, mix your own. I use equal parts of well-rotted manure, fine peat moss, sand and ordinary soil from my garden.

Container soil needs to be renewed annually, just like garden soil. Dump half the soil from each container into a large garbage can, renew it using the above formula, then remix it with the remaining half. Do this in the fall if you can, and never on the same day that you plant. The soil will need time to settle.

In most towns and cities, finding a source of topsoil to purchase is not a great problem. All you have to do is look in the yellow pages or check the classified ads in the local newspaper. But from there, it gets tricky. Most soil suppliers deliver in large trucks, and you often pay for the size of the truck the merchant happens to own rather than for the soil. Quite frequently, the merchant is really just a guy with a dump truck, and he knows and cares a lot more about his truck than about what he will be dumping in your yard. There is no way to guarantee that you're going to get good topsoil, but there are some basic rules you can follow.

The most important rule is that cheapest does not mean best. Where I live, most of the cheap available soil comes from the nearby river delta. These soils look great, but they are heavy, acidic and often full of exotic weeds. The first load I bought for my garden was of the cheap variety. On the telephone, the supplier naturally claimed that it was weed-free, which, judging from his appearance when he arrived, probably meant that he hadn't mixed any marijuana into it. The problem was that it contained most of the other known weeds on the continent. Worse, it came in solid lumps and it was so acidic that it would dissolve anything but thick rubber boots. Bringing it up to scratch, which I had to do by adding large amounts of lime, sand and fertilizers, was a major headache.

When I bought my second load, I was smarter. I drove to a reputable garden-supply company to see what their soil was like and what they did to it. If you can get a look at the soil before you buy it, I encourage you to do so. You may save yourself a load of grief. Even though my second load cost me more than double the price per cubic yard of the first, the humus, sand and nutrients were properly balanced, and in the end, it was a better buy. I haven't regretted paying the extra money, just as I haven't regretted buying decent tires for my car. You get what you pay for.

In some areas, acid rain is a major problem, and surface soils tend to be acidic wherever they are, even when they come from atop a limestone quarry. You will have to add generous amounts of lime as you dig this kind of soil into your own. That will save time and spare you a great measure of unhappiness in the long run. Unless you've bought top-grade manufactured soil, as I did with my second load, your new topsoil will probably require lime and fertilizers, since it has probably been derelict for years. In urban areas, that means it will be acidic. If you can afford bonemeal, use that to sweeten the soil. I use my own cheaper mixture of dolomitic (slow-acting) lime, bonemeal, manure and a chemical fertilizer such as 4-10-10 or 10-6-6 (see page 39 for an explanation of these designations).

If you have the energy, dig most of the new topsoil under your existing topsoil at the outset, then double-dig (see page 32) the entire plot. This will be hard work, but it will ensure that you have broken the subsurface of your existing garden and that you are not merely dumping new soil on top of compacted soil as impermeable as your driveway. If you don't do it at the start, you'll probably end up doing it later on when it will be twice as much work. Don't forget to give the old soil the additional humus and lime it needs when you do this. Chances are it will need even more revitalization and balancing than the new soil.

□ SPECIAL PROBLEMS

You literally never know what you'll find in your garden. The most common things are rocks. My guideline is that anything larger than a golf ball should be removed. If the rocks are big enough, use them for the rock garden or for drainage under sidewalks and patios.

Unless you're very lucky, you will also find other buried treasures. Until surprisingly recently, people often buried their garbage on their own property. If you find patches of broken glass and other detritus, get rid of it. If the debris isn't too dense, sift it from the soil and discard it.

Old sidewalks are another problem, particularly if your soil building involves major revisions of existing or decayed landscaping. I broke the old sidewalks at my house into small chunks and buried them beneath my new sidewalks along with some drainage pipes and gravel. That gave me some additional garden space and helped improve the drainage in new garden plots.

☐ OPTIMUM SOIL TYPES

In general, vegetables, particularly root crops, prefer a slightly lighter soil than do most other plantings. Soil composition is the main parameter, but the pH level—the relative acidity of the soil—is also important. Coniferous shrubs and trees, rhododendrons and azaleas, for instance, need acidic soils in order to thrive. The acid levels they require are high enough to make them incompatible with many other plant species, so you will have to choose between them and a lot of others. In the vegetable garden, potatoes can cause similar problems. Low acid content can cause potatoes to be bony (when cooked, they are mushy on the outside but raw inside). In a small garden, this means that you have to create a special bed for them—with all the attendant problems entailed in doing so.

Sandy loam—soil with lots of humus and sand in it—is optimal for growing nearly everything. As it turns out, it really doesn't matter how dark the soil is either. The dark colour simply marks the presence of well-rotted peat moss. While it is usually rich in humus, black soil comes from a location that was once a bog or swamp, so it might need a jolt of sand to loosen it up and some lime to sweeten it. Soil for perennial plots really ought to have extra-generous amounts of humus, if only because you won't have the opportunity to dig more into the lower depths each year

as you do with an annual flower or vegetable plot.

☐ FROM TURF TO GARDEN

Whether you are rebuilding a decayed garden, starting a new one in an established lot or simply enlarging an existing one, you're almost always going to have to remove and dispose of grass turf. Unfortunately, there's no easy transition from lawn to productive garden. In fact, I think there's only one way to do it.

I've had an unusual amount of experience with this problem, since I seem to have made something of a career of building gardens in yards that have been in turf for decades. Over time, I've developed a method that seems to work better than anything else I've heard of. The only problem is that it involves a lot of work.

The first rule is that there are no shortcuts. You must remove the turf. Under no circumstances should you rent a rototiller and grind it up. If you do, your garden will not do well, and it will be back in grass within a couple of years. The second rule is that you must wear heavy gardening gloves: you're going to get blisters, and this way, they won't be so painful.

☐ The Not-Especially-Easy but Best Grass-to-Garden Method

Let's assume that you have a good-sized patch of lawn that you want to make into a garden—say, a plot 10 feet by 10 feet. You will need only two tools for this, at least initially: a very good long-handled spade with a sharp blade and a good-quality shovel. I use a file to keep my spade extra sharp.

1. Divide the plot into one-foot squares with your spade, pushing it in to a depth of three to four inches, enough to cut beneath the roots of the grass.

2. Using the spade like a horizontal cleaver, cut just below the roots of the grass. Take out a 1-by-10-foot row of squares, and stack them close by. Then take out the adjacent 1-by-10-

DOUBLE DIGGING

The method of burying turf that I have described is a practice with general application throughout a small-lot garden, particularly with raised beds. Double digging is hard work, but there's nothing terribly complicated about it, and it is truly worth the extra effort.

I try to double-dig all my nonperennial beds every two or three years. The best time is late summer or early fall before the autumn rains make the soil too heavy. If your climate gives you a very short period between harvest and freeze-up, do it in the spring.

The basic technique is to dig down two shovel depths instead of the conventional one. Double digging will allow easy root penetration to a greater depth, and the compost you shovel in at the bottom will give the plants a feast when their roots reach it. Double digging is valuable for both vegetable gardens and annual flowerbeds.

In the author's backyard, the narrow, bordered pathways provide deep access to the raised beds. Note the clever use of six-mil plastic to create protective tents over lettuce seedlings.

foot strip, and stack those squares too.
3. Once you've cleared a 2-by-10-foot patch, use your shovel to dig down 18 inches or to just below the plane of the subsoil (whichever comes first) and remove all the soil. Stack the soil on the grass at the end of the plot. (If you have a sheet of heavy plastic or a tarpaulin, lay that down along the side of the plot, and stack the soil on it to keep the soil from burying the remaining grass.) You will now have a reasonably neat pit about 18 inches deep on one edge of your new garden.
4. Drop the squares of turf face down into the pit so that they line the bottom. Throw a couple of handfuls of dolomitic lime on top of the squares, along with several handfuls of 10-5-5 fertilizer and anything you have lying around that is organic but not woody, such as leaves or kitchen scraps—but no meat. (Remember to wear those

thick gardening gloves so that the fertilizer won't get into your blisters.) The lime and fertilizer will help break down the turf more quickly and will give your soil a feeding at its lowest levels.
5. Shovel the year's compost into the bottom of the pit to a depth of three to six inches, whether the compost is mature or not. It will finish decaying there. After screening the soil you've dug out for stones and rocks, mix it with peat moss and well-rotted manure, if you have any, in roughly equal proportions. I do this in a wheelbarrow. Then pour it into the pit to a level several inches above the ground.
6. Remove another 2-by-10-foot strip of sod, stack the pieces on the side, and repeat steps 3, 4 and 5 until the entire 10-by-10-foot plot has been stripped of sod and dug down and the sod has been limed, fertilized and buried.
7. Take a break from gardening for a

few days while your back recovers. Rave to your friends about what a terrific garden you're going to have. Go to your chiropractor and have your spinal column put back into alignment, but do not tell him or her what you've been doing. Chiropractors often don't understand gardeners.

What I've just described is extremely hard work. If you do, in fact, have a back problem, it would make a lot of sense to hire a sturdy neighbourhood teenager to do the work for you. Just be sure to supervise the project carefully, because as I've already said, it is one that allows no shortcuts.

☐ *An Important Note*

Before you bury turf, check it for weeds. If there aren't any – none at all – then in all probability, the grass has recently been subjected to selective herbicides that are toxic to broadleaf plants but not to grass. If this is the case, you're faced with some choices. Herbicides of this type do not permanently affect broadleaf plant growth; the longevity of their ability to cause health problems in people and animals, however, is far less certain.

One option is to haul such turf to the dump, in which case, you make it a public problem. Another is to lime and stack it on your own property and let nature break the herbicides down as far as it can. If you have a side yard you don't use, stack the turf there and leave it for a couple of years, with plastic under and over it to keep the herbicides from leaching out. I did that to a suspicious patch of turf which I successfully used later as a base for some flowerbed landscaping. It can also be used as a deep base for tree plantings after it has sat for a while. These are ways of not passing one's own problems on to

Freestanding raised beds (those not rigidly contained by wooden or cement borders) give the vegetable gardener planting flexibility from year to year as well as from season to season. Make sure you create pathways between the beds for watering, weeding and harvesting, and remember that any number of flowers other than marigolds can be planted nearby.

everyone else. There aren't any clean, simple options. Given the environmental mess we are in, the choice is between selfishly safe and responsibly unsafe.

☐ *Landscaping and Raised Beds*

Once you start digging your garden, you will probably hit subsoil before you reach a depth of 18 inches, and this means that you will have to add topsoil. You'll almost certainly need additional topsoil if you have just moved into a new house on a new lot. If you need to add more than 4 or 5 inches, you will have what may appear to be a small planning crisis on your hands: your garden is going to be substantially higher than the adjoining parts of the yard.

Happily, this often solves more problems than it creates. If you have a high water table, nothing could be better, because the increased soil height will improve drainage. Even if the water table is not a problem, raising your garden beds offers some significant advantages that you can profit by.

In the 1960s and 1970s, it was both fashionable and economically necessary for many of us to simply plunk an old mattress or a piece of foam on the floor and sleep on that. In that period, I contracted pneumonia several years in a row. I assumed then that it was what is now called a "life-style consequence," because many of my friends also had pneumonia on a regular basis. One year, I built a loft and began sleeping some six feet from the floor. I abruptly ceased to get pneumonia. I realized then that it had been drafty and cold down on the floor and not at all good for my health.

Some of my friends don't believe this theory of mine has any scientific basis, and they get thoroughly irate when I suggest that sleeping on the floor is not good for them. To dispel their doubts, I wrote letters to the World Health Organization (WHO) and to the National Aeronautics and Space Administration (NASA) to see whether they could confirm my theory. I never did get an answer. I guess the WHO was too busy fighting famines and NASA too busy destroying the ozone layer with space shuttles. Finally, I asked my mother about it, and she confirmed the truth of my theory instantly. "Why do you think parrots live so much longer than muskrats?" she asked.

Isn't science wonderful?

Whether or not we can scientifically prove that raised beds prevent pneumonia and a host of other student diseases, nearly every garden expert will tell you that they are a perfect solution to a variety of problems in compact gardens. I first encountered this method of gardening in sufficient detail for it to be helpful about 11 years ago in a book by Peter Chan called *Better Vegetable Gardens the Chinese Way*. It took me some time to separate Chan's mysticism from his highly practical technical procedures, and in the meantime, I discovered that European gardeners, who have a wealth of experience with gardening in restricted quarters, have also been using the raised-bed technique for centuries.

There are many good reasons for building raised beds in a small garden. They encourage intensive plantings, and properly constructed, they add symmetry and neatness to a yard. More important, the soil in raised beds warms earlier in the spring, drainage and soil aeration are better than in ordinary beds and a more even moisture level can be maintained.

The ideal raised bed is roughly four feet wide, although it can be of any length. This allows for convenient cultivation, weeding and harvesting from either side of the bed without your having to step on and pack down the soil as you work. If you want raised beds along the edge of your property, make them narrower. I built my raised beds out of a combination of railway ties and 2-by-10 planks, mainly because I happened to have both available. If I were richer, I'd have used treated 4-by-12s, but these are pretty expensive. I was also lucky enough to come upon a free supply of used bricks to put in between the beds, but stones or even sawdust or plain old soil will do almost as well. If you have the inclination and the money, you can pour concrete or have somebody else do it for you. Just make sure you're happy with the design and location first, because poured concrete is a fairly permanent feature. It is also about as biodegradable as uranium and a lot bulkier.

THE CARE AND FEEDING OF GARDENS

Some people assume that the more they feed a garden, the better it will grow—a very dangerous assumption, because nothing could be further from the truth. Plants need to be fed carefully, and each plant species has its own optimum diet. An overfed plant does not turn into a fat, productive glutton. More often than not, it starts looking like some other kind of plant. And frequently, it gets sick and keels over.

Listed below are the six building blocks of plant nutrition.

□ *Sunlight*: An obvious component, but it is a good idea to remember that different plants prefer different intensities and durations of sunlight and that some of them are not flexible about it.

□ *Water*: Also an obvious component, but again, requirements vary from one plant to another. Overwatering and untimely or inappropriate watering can cause as many problems as no watering at all.

□ *Nitrogen*: Nitrogen is for leafy growth and great for leafy vegetables and grass, but too much of it will burn the leaves of most plants.

□ *Phosphorus*: The root builder. When a plant's roots are not adequate, the plant will not thrive. This applies to nearly everything in life and is especially true in your garden.

□ *Potassium*: The stem builder. Every plant has a complex transit network linking the foliage, which draws energy from the sun to conduct photosynthesis, with the roots, which supply the nutrients and most of the moisture for photosynthesis. Potassium builds the highways and bridges for this essential commerce.

□ *Humus*: Humus is decayed organic material, and it is the medium that allows plant roots to absorb and use nutrients. Depending on what the source of humus is, it will contain varying amounts of nitrogen, potassium and phosphorus. Animal manure, of which there are a number of types, is the most common form. But compost, leaves, seaweed, lake weed, straw and a number of other organic materials also do the trick. If your soil is humus-poor, then all the fertilizers in the universe won't help you.

Additionally, plants require a wide variety of trace elements for healthy growth; among them are copper, boron, magnesium and sulphur. Too much of some of them will cause problems because they are all toxic if present in volume. Their absence will also cause problems. Humus-rich soils, particularly those supplemented with household compost, are rarely short on trace elements, and compost is the preferred method of providing them.

□ CHEMICAL VERSUS ORGANIC FERTILIZERS

Some gardeners object on principle to the use of chemical fertilizers, arguing that chemicals are dangerous to human health, that chemical fertilizers are really petrochemicals and that they can burn plants. On the other hand, they are convenient and allow for specific and disease-free feeding of crops.

My opinion? I use chemical fertilizers. I think that many of the arguments against them are inconsistent at best and hypocritical at worst. For one thing, overapplication of a concentrated organic fertilizer can burn plants just as easily as a chemical equivalent can. For

CREOSOTE AND CANCER

I am not a doctor, a cancer researcher or a soil scientist, so I have no definite answers to the ongoing controversy surrounding the carcinogenic properties of decay retardants such as creosote and the substances used in pressure-treated (green) lumber. I have old railway ties in my garden, so if they are dangerous to health, I've been in danger for about 10 years now.

As part of my research for this book, I attempted to ascertain the facts in this controversy, and as far as I can determine, there are no solid facts. There are several theories, many rumours and some near-facts. One part of me believes, perhaps cynically, that every substance on the planet is going to be the subject, sooner or later, of a cancer-hysteria scare. Nonetheless, if the rumours ever turn out to have substance and if the near-facts get much firmer, I will get rid of my railway ties. If you are worried about the potential hazards, don't use ties for the vegetable garden. Unless you're into making salads with flower blossoms, using railway ties likely won't hurt you anywhere else in the garden.

another, those who righteously eschew commercial petrochemical fertilizers commonly use rock phosphate, which is almost identical in composition to its petrochemical equivalent but is mined from natural rock. Is strip mining somehow more virtuous than an oil well?

The claims chemical-fertilizer manufacturers make about their products are largely true: they are convenient, and they carry no diseases. But most of them do not contain the trace elements common in organic compounds or in compost, and most important, they contain no humus. For me, it is not an either-or kind of question. A sensible approach is to use both, and I have a distinct preference for organic fertilizers.

□   *Organic Fertilizers*

An abundance of organic fertilizers is available to home gardeners. Most are relatively inexpensive, and some are even free. The commercial ones, however, are sometimes overpriced, particularly if they come in liquid form. Before you buy these, check the labels carefully; often, they aren't entirely organic. Look around to see whether you can find free equivalents easily. Organic fertilizers that come in bulk are generally good value because they are doing two jobs at once: they provide nutrients and humus at the same time. Here is a list of organic fertilizers.

□   *Manures*

I have a fondness for manure that I can't quite explain, except to speculate that perhaps an organic gardener lurks somewhere in my soul. One of my areas of agreement with the organic-gardening industry is with its dismay at the way North Americans fail to recycle biological wastes. It is abundantly clear to me that if we don't improve our methods fairly soon, we aren't going to be here to improve them later on. A rule to observe with any animal manure: the older it is, the better it will be.

□ *Steer manure:* Steer manure is a polite but slightly inaccurate term for cattle droppings mixed with wood shavings and composted for several years. I mean, really, the cows are in on this too—and, presumably, some bulls. Steer manure is relatively cheap and readily available in easy-to-handle plastic bags, but it is not always as sterile as it is claimed to be, and it is frequently much more raw than advertised. It has a distinct and rather unpleasant odour, and among animal manures, it carries the fewest nutrients.

□ *Chicken manure:* Even the commercial varieties of chicken manure have a high ammonia content, which means that chicken manure is loaded with nitrogen. It is good stuff, even in raw form, but it can burn plants very easily if you apply it carelessly. I compost raw chicken manure for a few months before I put it on my garden.

□ *Horse manure:* I think horse manure is superior to the others. My reason for saying this is more a matter of aesthetics than of science. I admire horses, and I think the odour of their manure is rather pleasant. Well-rotted horse manure is often very expensive and rare, because most of it is now used for mushroom production. I actually prefer to go out to the horse barns and collect it myself. That allows me to meet the horses that produced the manure. Be sure to get manure mixed with straw, not with wood shavings, which are acidic, take a long time to break down and can be toxic to plants. Don't lay raw horse manure directly onto the garden. Add it to the compost pile, where it will do double duty as an activator for other decomposing organic materials.

□ *Mushroom manure:* Where I live, this kind of manure is quite easy to obtain. It is actually worn-out horse manure that has been used as a medium for growing mushrooms. There aren't great amounts of nutrients left by the time you get it, but it makes a great soil conditioner. I hear that mushroom growers typically get their manure from the horse barns at racetracks, so mushroom manure may make your plants grow faster and become more graceful.

□ *Green manure*: Did you know that you can manufacture your own manure? And no, it isn't what you think. (Human fecal wastes are undesirable in the garden for a number of reasons, as is the dung of any carnivore, cats and dogs included. The main reason is the possible presence of harmful *E. coli* bacteria and other pathogens.) Green manure is created by sowing a crop such as alfalfa, winter rye or white navy beans in your empty vegetable beds after harvest and then digging it under in the late fall or early spring. A lot of gardeners swear by it, and I have used it myself several times.

□ *Getting and Using Manure*

You can purchase several kinds of bagged manure from supermarkets and garden shops, but that isn't really the preferred method. A trip to the local horse barns or to a chicken farm (which may put you off eating eggs) can be an interesting weekend outing, particularly if you have small children.

If you can locate a large supply of well-aged manure, you might try buying a truckload of it cooperatively with your neighbours. We did that in our back alley one fall, and after the trucker dumped it smack in the middle of the alley, we all scurried around getting it into our gardens as fast as we could. The Chinese family didn't own a wheelbarrow, but they got their fair share anyway: grandparents, parents, aunts, uncles and children as young as 4 and 5 years old hauled it away in pails and buckets. If you're going to get a large quantity of manure, though, my best advice is that you don't buy it sight unseen. One person I know who did that ended up with 10 cubic yards of wood shavings spiced with an occasional raw cowpie. If you're buying it by the load, get it in the fall and dig most of it in as soon as you can, but make sure you save some for the compost pile.

The only manure I put directly onto the garden is green manure. I compost other manures—even the bagged varieties—for at least a few months and let the bacteria they provide speed the rest of my compost along. For some reason, this seems to do away with the unpleasant odours of steer manure.

□ *Seaweed and Lake Weed*

If you're lucky enough to live near the ocean, you have available to you one of the best multipurpose organic substances around, and all you have to do is go down to the beach after a good storm and scoop it up. I do, several times a year. Wash seaweed down well with the hose before using it, though, because the salt is not good for your soil. Seaweed makes a good mulch, particularly for tomatoes. I dig it into the garden in the fall as a soil conditioner or dump it onto the compost heap. It has a high potassium content, something animal manures are usually a bit light on.

If you live inland, lake weed is a valuable resource with similar properties. Where my parents live now, imported Eurasian milfoil weed has become an enormous problem in nearby lakes and waterways—to everyone except my father. He scoops up whatever he can find along the lakeshores and digs it directly into his garden.

□ *Other Organic Fertilizers*

Fish and seaweed fertilizers are receiving a lot of attention these days, but frankly, I don't quite understand why. I am not a big fan of any kind of spray fertilizer, and the fish- or seaweed-based liquid fertilizers are stinky and expensive. Some of them aren't completely organic either. They are actually chemical concoctions to which a seaweed concentrate has been added to provide trace elements.

Bonemeal and blood meal are wonderful substances for the dedicated organic gardener. Unfortunately, they are also extremely expensive. Consequently, I use bonemeal only for bulbs, tree plantings and perennial-bed preparation. I'd use it for a lot more applications if it weren't so expensive. I have never used blood meal. The idea of it is pretty gross, and besides, I've heard it is excellent slug food. Use it on your Venus' fly traps and other carnivorous plants.

☐ *Chemical Fertilizers*

Each of the large number of chemical fertilizers on the market today has its particular uses, but they should be used very, very carefully. If you use them in concentrated pure form, add another "very" to the caution. All chemicals are capable of burning your plants. If you want to experience what a plant might be feeling, stick your bare hand into a bag of chemical fertilizer for about 15 seconds. It isn't exactly pleasant.

Below are the basic formulations in which chemical fertilizers are sold. The first digit always denotes the nitrogen content, the second phosphorus and the third potash.

☐ *10-6-6*: An all-purpose fertilizer for flowers, vegetables and spring application to the lawn. It's a satisfactory formula, but I use it only for the compost heap, which requires a little more nitrogen than the garden does.

☐ *4-10-10*: This one is good for vegetables and flowers, and I use it more than any other.

☐ *6-8-6*: I just don't like this one as much as some of the others. I have no scientific reason; I prefer to supply nitrogen organically.

☐ *3-15-6*: This is bulb food, useful for flowering bulbs, onions and garlic. Buy it in small packages, and drop whatever you haven't used during the year onto the carrot bed in the fall.

☐ *Liquid Chemicals*

Although they are a little easier to store than granular fertilizers, I try not to use liquid chemicals at all in the garden. They are appropriate for houseplants, but even with those, I prefer to mix my own feeding solution 20-20-20 from powder. With liquids, you wind up paying quite a lot for their water content, and since almost anyone — myself included — is capable of mixing things with water, I don't see the point of them. There's one exception: a solution called 0-10-10 works sensationally with potted flowering outdoor plants like geraniums and petunias, particularly late in the summer.

☐ MULCHING

Mulching can be a very useful technique for conserving soil moisture, particularly in areas where the summers are hot and dry. But in many climates and gardening locations — mine, for instance — it simply doesn't make sense, and as far as I can see, it never makes as much sense as the mulching maniacs say it does. Mulching rests currently in that grey area between functionality and fashion. Some gardeners claim so many benefits for mulching that one gets the feeling that they'd mulch their cars or their mothers if they could.

After that introduction, perhaps I had better tell you just what mulching is. Mulching is the application of different materials to the soil's surface in order to preserve moisture, provide nutrients, suppress weed growth and guard against insect damage. In an optimum situation, mulching would achieve at least some of these goals, particularly that of conserving soil moisture and suppressing weed growth, although I have never understood how it could fend off insect attacks. Maybe the attacking insects get lost on the way to their targets.

Inappropriately applied, mulch can keep the soil from warming properly, and it can provide an excellent breeding ground for diseases and insects. Earwigs and slugs, for instance, thrive in mulch. Another drawback is that rotting organic material also has a tendency to rob the soil of nitrogen.

Contrary to rumour, mulching is no protection at all from UFO attacks. It may even encourage them. Most UFO sightings take place in the midwestern United States, where there are both an overabundance of straw and a lot of fanatical mulchers.

□ *Organic Mulches*

The most common and probably most useful mulch is straw, which is available in cities directly from farmers or from very chic garden shops. Be careful that what you're getting is straw —the stems of grain crops—and not hay, which is harvested from wild and domestic grasses. Straw is coarser in appearance and is relatively free of seeds. Hay is loaded with seeds, and using it will have about the same effect as sowing grass seed across your garden —not a recommended procedure.

Seaweed and lake weed, to my mind, are superior mulches, and they are free for the picking in many areas. They carry no garden weeds, break down slightly faster than straw and contain quite a few more valuable soil nutrients. If you're using seaweed, be sure to wash the salt from it with the hose before laying it down.

Grass clippings can also be used for mulching, as can sawdust, wood shavings and leaves. However, I don't recommend any of them, because all have a tendency to leach nitrogen from the soil, particularly sawdust and wood shavings. I would be very cautious with using either of those for any application in the garden. They're acidic, and some tree species, such as cedar, can be mildly toxic to other plant species.

If, despite my attempts to dissuade you, you're determined to mulch anyway, look around you. I know someone who lives next door to a peanut butter factory and has been using peanut hulls as both compost and mulch material for nearly a decade, with excellent results.

□ *Inorganic Mulches*

The most common inorganics used as mulch are black plastic and Reemay, which is a fine netting material. Both provide a wonderful breeding ground for all kinds of bugs and diseases if your climate is damp. So do old newspapers, which are organic except for some of the inks used to print them. Mulching experts will caution you not to use newspapers with coloured ink, which is said to be toxic. If you can figure out a way to keep the newspapers from scattering in the wind (I never have, short of putting a lot of bricks on top of them, which defeats the purpose) and if you're willing to sort the coloured pages from those with black ink, go ahead and mulch with newspapers. You'll be surprised to see how much of your local newspaper now contains coloured ink. And your neighbours are going to think you are a little unstable.

Personally, I don't think inorganic materials of any kind should be used in the garden when there's an alternative, which there almost always is. So I've never used plastic mulches, except once, when I found a big sheet of eight-mil black plastic on an abandoned construction site. I used it to make soil caps around some cauliflower I was trying to grow. It worked fine for a few weeks— until the slugs that were using it as a day-care centre got hungry and went looking for groceries.

To be fair, I have to admit that my prejudice against mulches may not be entirely justified. The climate where I live is wetter than most, and my attitude probably reflects that a little more than it should. I'm willing to concede that in semiarid climates, mulching is really very useful, perhaps even a necessity. And I do use mulches for specific applications. Tomatoes seem to like a seaweed mulch during the summer heat, and I sometimes use six-mil plastic in the spring as a cover to let soil dry. My Chinese neighbours use sheets of cardboard to keep soil moisture off their squashes and melons in early spring and late summer. But I will stick by my conviction that mulches shouldn't be used indiscriminately and that they don't cure all garden ills in one fell swoop. Incidentally, you should always wear

An unpainted, open picket fence

surrounds this mixed garden, which

features raised beds made of foot-

deep planks and plantings of onions,

lettuce and perennial and annual herbs.

The mulched pathways provide access

and prevent weeds from taking over.

a checked shirt while mulching. And watch out for UFOs.

☐ COMPOSTING

I have no skepticism whatsoever about compost, and people who have had the pleasure of running their fingers through a bucket of mature compost they have produced themselves will know why. Aside from the considerable benefits to the garden, producing compost makes you a little wiser about how the world works and a little more tolerant of life's ostensibly cruel processes. It is also a responsible method of recycling some of the massive quantities of food we waste.

But let's not get too spiritual about it. Compost is a valuable friend to your garden. Mature compost is perhaps the finest soil builder available. When you make and use it, you not only become a spiritually correct recycler, you will obtain a source of humus and fertilizer that is particularly rich in trace elements. Remember, though, that its primary purpose is to provide humus to your soil, not fertilizer.

For a gardener working in a garden of limited size, composting can create some difficulties. It takes up a fair amount of valuable garden space, and unless you're careful, it can give off a few odours your neighbours may not appreciate. It can also attract vermin. Fortunately, there are ways to get around these problems if you exercise some common sense.

□ *Handling Compost*

Put your compost bins in a sheltered spot in the back garden that isn't too far out of the way yet is not where your neighbours will see or smell it. To my mind, it's best to build a double- or triple-bin system, which will allow one batch of prepared compost to percolate its way to rich maturity undisturbed while the second and third are being concocted. Be sure to build your bins so that the compost can be conveniently turned and removed. A number of commercial composters are also currently available, and more are coming onto the market every day. Most of the ones I've had a look at so far are sort of funny-looking and inefficient—round in shape and made out of inorganic plastics. They're okay, I suppose, but remember that you'll need at least two of them, that they're relatively expensive and that a good compost bin is not difficult or expensive to build on your own.

If you want to get elaborate about composting, you can easily get plans for some really exotic (and scientific) composting systems. A browse through almost any gardening periodical will turn up one or two. *Organic Gardening* magazine seems to come up with at least half a dozen new systems a year, and each one claims to solve most of the problems of the world while making compost faster than the blink of an eye.

If you go this route, be prepared to spend at least four hours a week fooling around with them, and get your food processor ready to help chew the compost materials down to size.

You can alter your system to fit available space, but try to maintain the fundamental principles. Compost needs some ventilation, a moderate but even supply of moisture, some nitrogen and a midrange pH balance. It also likes to be turned from time to time. You do not absolutely have to turn compost, but if you don't, it will take longer to mature, and in a small garden, swift maturation is an important consideration.

□ *The Black-Bag Compost Method*

If you have the kind of garden that does not produce much excess vegetation (or if you live entirely on canned food or TV dinners), you can produce compost very quickly by filling a plastic garbage bag with a mélange of finely shredded vegetable material, a bucketful of commercial steer manure and a handful of 10-6-6 mixed with some lime. A friend of mine does this, chopping her organic kitchen scraps in her food processor, and she produces bags of first-rate compost quite regularly. No further comment is required, except that the in-

If you have the space, a permanent three-bin composter will serve you well (one bin in process, one for new stuff and one to use). If you're building the composter yourself, try to use scrap materials to save costs (cedar or pressure-treated wood will last longer). Also, use galvanized nails, which don't rust, and make sure your side boards and front slats provide adequate ventilation. Otherwise, the compost will drown or become starved for air. Remember to make the front slats removable, or you'll have to dismantle the entire thing to get the mature compost out.

organic bags rarely survive more than one production cycle and that I think she ought to be institutionalized.

□ *Working With Worms*

I have at least one idiosyncrasy of my own in making compost. I read, some time ago, about the function of earthworms in producing compost, and I'm convinced that the value of the little wrigglers can't be overestimated. Each spring as I spade the garden, I collect all the earthworms I find and transfer them to the compost heap. I am especially careful to remove them from wherever I intend to plant root crops, because I add 5 percent granular diazinon with the seed. The diazinon does in root maggots and carrot rust fly larvae, and it will also kill any earthworms that happen to be in the vicinity.

If you have small children, set them to work gathering the worms. If you explain to them why they are doing it, they will enjoy the work, and besides saving the worms' lives and improving your compost, they will learn not to be finicky. The worms you put in the compost will also provide another service: if they stay there, you have the best possible indicator that your compost has a good pH balance and an adequate amount of air. If they leave, you'll know that you have a problem.

□ *A Checklist of Compostable Materials*

□ *All uncooked kitchen vegetable scraps*: Kitchen scraps are loaded with trace elements, so keep a bucket in your kitchen to collect them. Citrus fruit peels are highly acidic, so add a spoonful of lime to your compost bucket. As a general rule, I don't put anything that's been cooked in my compost. I use salt in cooking, which is very bad for the garden, and earthworms don't like it. They don't like cooking oils or butter either, although rats and mice do.
□ *Coffee grounds and tea leaves, including tea bags*: Coffee grounds can help to deodorize the compost, but they're acidic,

so as with citrus waste, you'll have to compensate with lime. If you make your coffee with unbleached filters, toss the filters in with the coffee grounds.
□ *All vegetation from the garden that is not diseased or woody*: This includes weeds, as long as they have not flowered. If you even suspect that a garden plant is diseased, toss it into the garbage can. I do not compost woody plants — twigs, branches or shrub prunings. They will compost, but they take longer than I'm prepared to wait. If I happen to think of it, I sometimes stick them in the barbecue and then collect the ashes for the compost. (In most cities, including mine, burning this stuff is illegal.)
□ *Grass clippings*: Use only clippings that don't come from a lawn that has had a fertilizer-weed-killer mixture used on it. Fresh grass clippings will temporarily help to heat the compost, but when you add a good load of clippings, a handful of nitrogen-rich fertilizer will keep them from robbing the compost of the nitrogen so crucial to microorganism activity. A few days later, turn the clippings into the rest of the compost because they have a tendency to layer.
□ *Autumn leaves*: Leaves make an excellent soil builder, but they contain surprisingly few soil nutrients and should be shredded and mixed with other organics to facilitate breakdown. I collect my own, and from time to time, I put the kids in the car and go rake leaves in the public parks. I get the humus, and the city gets a minor public service. The public works departments of some of the more forward-looking cities now compost leaves each fall and use them the following spring in their public parks. Most still dump them into landfills. If your city does that, complain loudly.

Never put wrecked cars, explosives or defeated governments in your compost heap.

□ *Layering and Turning Compost*

Just filling your compost bins with organic material will not make compost

—not quickly, anyway. The best compost is produced by a combination of four basic materials that should, initially at least, be placed in the compost in layers. Different experts will give you different combinations, and I'm not sure which is the best one. If I am going through one of my infrequent organized phases, I let a four-to-six-inch layer of vegetable materials build up and then add a handful of mixed dolomitic lime and chemical fertilizer (10-6-6 is best, and it is optional), over which I drop a two-to-four-inch layer of mixed soil and manure. When the next layer of vegetable material has accumulated, I turn it into the previous two and begin again.

There are also compost-activating products on the market, but I don't use them. I bought one small package a few years ago and took it apart. As far as I could see, it was nothing more than a mixture of the same lime and chemical fertilizers I use but at four times the price.

When I remember, I cover the compost bins against the rain. It's quite easy to let your compost heap drown.

◻ *PESTS, DISEASES AND WEEDS*
Trying to tell you exactly which pests, diseases and weeds are going to be your particular problem would be misleading, since all three vary widely from neighbourhood to neighbourhood and from one soil type to another, let alone from one geographical region to another. There is one thing I can say for sure on the subject, however: urban and suburban gardeners, particularly those who garden in compact spaces, have greater problems with pests, diseases and weeds than are found in any other kind of agriculture.

The reasons for this are not that difficult to figure out. Cities are perfect breeding grounds for plant diseases and insects. More species of plants are grown in cities than on farms or in uncultivated environments, and they are grown in closer proximity to one another. Since each species has its own unique set of diseases and insect susceptibilities, there's a good chance that they'll end up in your garden. Likewise, weeds are very hard to control, because you can't control what your neighbours grow, intentionally or unintentionally, and because much of what ought to be common space in cities—roads, rights-of-way and vacant spaces—has become derelict or forbidden ground. Even the topsoil and manure you add to your original soils carry the risk of new pests and diseases, particularly if you aren't sure where the topsoil came from.

Unfortunately, there is not much you can do about it. These enemies of the garden are facts of urban life, as are buses, good restaurants, art galleries, noisy muscle-cars, foul-mouthed strangers, drunks in the park and the occasional prowler lurking in the alley. Cities are a mixed bag, and you have to live with the mix as best you can. I do, however, have four rules for dealing with insect pests, diseases and weeds.
◻ I do use pesticides, but very carefully and only on specific crops at specific times. Wherever possible, I use organically based insecticides or insecticidal soap sprays.
◻ I use no herbicides whatsoever. I don't see any convincing reason to use fertilizer-weed-killer combinations on the lawn, and I see lots of reasons not to. If you have a really outrageous outbreak of dandelions or trailing buttercups, you can use a specific weed killer that is not a spray and kills the offenders off one at a time. I still think you're better off to pick them out by hand with a screwdriver or a nail puller.
◻ Keep moving your vegetable crops around the garden on a four-year cycle. I do not grow any of the cabbage family in my garden because the load of cheap topsoil I brought in a few years ago had clubroot virus in it. My neighbours seem to be able to grow cabbages, but I've put a four-year quarantine on my garden, and I have a feeling even that won't get rid of the virus.
◻ I weed often and ruthlessly. First of

◻   ◻   ◻   ◻   ◻

COMPOST SHREDDERS

I'm not the kind of person who will use the kitchen blender or food processor to shred compost, but last summer, I did buy one of those small hand-powered compost shredders often advertised in seed catalogues. It works fine—sort of. It shreds almost anything you put into it about as well as you'd want, but it does so very, very slowly, and it cost far too much for what it can actually accomplish.

It looks quite nice sitting by the compost bin, though. Nearly every one of my neighbours has gravely asked me about it, even though they all know exactly what it is and what it does, because they've watched me in the garden jamming things into it and cursing quietly as I realize that it's taking all day.

Actually, an electric lawn mower will do the job almost as well, and it will do it much more quickly. I still use my lawn mower in the fall when large amounts of compostable material need to be prepared. Of course, you can buy an electric compost shredder. If you can afford one of those, you can probably also afford a gardener to electrocute himself while he's using it. In that case, you're likely reading the wrong book.

all, it's good exercise. I learned to be ruthless the hard way. A few years ago, I let several pigweed plants (nice people call it lamb's quarters or wild spinach) go to seed because I prefer the flavour of pigweed to that of spinach. The next year, I had an outbreak of leaf miners in my spinach and beet crops. Later on, I found out that the leaf miners winter in pigweed seeds.

Pesticides are a sad necessity for the small-lot city vegetable gardener. If you don't use them, you will simply lose much of your garden. But even if you use them carefully, you will almost certainly be getting small doses of possible carcinogens. I'm pretty sure that the doses you will get from your home-grown vegetables are smaller than those on the vegetables in supermarkets. Many of them have been heavily sprayed with chemicals so lethal that you can't obtain them for use in your garden even if you were crazy enough to want to use them.

When you do use pesticides, try to remember that not all the bugs in your garden are bad. Earthworms are your best allies, and they're highly sensitive to insecticides.

In British Columbia's rather moist climate, slugs are occasionally a real problem. But I don't put out slug bait, which cats and dogs seem to find delicious, and I don't, as some otherwise sane experts suggest, put out saucers of beer so that the slugs can get so drunk they forget about eating the plants.

I know this sounds unpleasant, but a trip through the garden just after dark with a flashlight, a small can and a four-inch spike will do in more slugs than 200 pounds of slug bait. It can get a bit messy on a busy night, but in the meantime, you'll get the best of the seasonal night aromas, and if you listen carefully, you can hear the plants growing. This method works well for caterpillar control too, since most of them feed at night. You will need a smaller nail or, better, an old pair of tweezers with which to pinch them.

Since insecticides and herbicides tend to accumulate in greater concentrations higher up the food chain, they're more of a danger to snakes, birds and other garden predators than they are to their intended victims. In the past two decades, scientists have developed pesticides that break down far more quickly than the earlier types, but it remains a matter of simple prudence to remember who is at the top of the food chain: people are.

□   *A NOTE ON ORGANIC GARDENING*

I admire organic gardeners for the many valuable gardening techniques they have pioneered or reintroduced. But when their ideas border on a religious faith in purity for its own sake, I begin to diverge. Like it or not, cities are not pure environments, and they are unlikely to become so without a degree of authoritarian control few North Americans seem prepared to accept. In addition, many of the more extreme organic-gardening techniques presuppose a rural environment, where crops can be widely separated, both from one another and from human intervention. If you are gardening on a small-to-moderate-sized city lot, you just can't employ those techniques, and I don't think you should feel guilty about it.

And while we're on the subject, I would counsel a certain wariness about the claims made for the purity of organic foods sold in most cities. Unsprayed crops are not usually allowed to cross borders, and it is a well-known fact that the general demand for "pure" foods far outstrips the productive capacities of small-scale local organic producers. I remember a story Lenny Bruce once told about a job he had working in the back room of an organic-food store in New York City, smearing chicken manure on store-bought eggs. I don't know if this still happens, but before I pay a premium price for pure foods, I want to be very sure I'm getting what I'm paying for.

THE EDIBLE GARDEN

The advantage of climbing plants is space efficiency. The beans, left, clamber up the fence, while the peas are supported with twine. Right: a ground-sunk pot of rosemary and a lattice-supported clematis.

My mother awakened my interest in vegetable gardening when I was about 6 years old, and that interest hasn't wavered since. In Prince George, British Columbia, where I grew up, vegetable gardening was a necessity, and most families had large kitchen gardens. California and Florida had not yet become the market gardens of the continent, and in the winter, sometimes the only fresh vegetables available to us were the storable ones grown locally. That meant a heavy reliance on crops such as carrots, cabbages, rutabagas, beets, onions and potatoes. In the late sum-mer, my mother did a lot of canning and pickling, so we always had beet pickles and a variety of cucumber pick-les on hand. Late every summer, fresh field tomatoes would be trucked in from the south, along with corn, pears, apples, apricots and peaches. I was a teenager before I saw such exotica as broccoli and Brussels sprouts and in my 20s before I encountered an avocado.

In Prince George, we couldn't grow corn or tomatoes because the season was too short, but we knew the differ-ence between canned corn and the real stuff, and we could distinguish between field tomatoes and those puny pink things the grocery stores sold in cellophane tubes. I got to like corn in pretty well any form, but really fresh corn on the cob has always been a cherished treat. To this day, I refuse to eat supermarket tomatoes, which have no taste whatsoever, and I avoid iceberg lettuce for the same reason.

Our interest in the flavour of vegetables was not the kind of interest a gourmet might have, but it was very much tied to quality-of-life issues. We wanted decent nutrition, and we wanted our food to have flavour. Consequently, fresh vegetables from the home garden were big events. We tended our vegetable gardens with care, and we celebrated the harvest with great delight and a certain degree of ceremony.

One of my family's ceremonies was the annual leaf-lettuce fight. It began each year with my mother bringing in the first leaves, washing them carefully and placing a large bowl of them on the dinner table. She would turn to one of my siblings and ask with great formality, "Do you know what this is?" Before the victim could answer the question, he or she would be slapped across the face with a dripping leaf of fresh lettuce, and the battle would be on.

The best of these summer garden rituals was the first garden stew. Because our season was short and very intense, much of what we grew — snap beans, onion sets, carrots and some potatoes — was ready at roughly the same time. My mother's way of celebrating the harvest was to make a stew. It was no minor deal either. For me, the occasion carried with it the same kind of joy that Christmas did.

Where I now live, the vegetables don't ripen all at once, and probably as a result, my stews never seem as good as my mother's did. But I still persist with this ceremony, occasionally to the considerable mystification of the friends invited over to partake of it. They just don't see why being invited to eat stew on a hot summer's evening is such an honour. Well, the answer is that being alive is an honour, and being able to grow and eat one's own vegetables is an honour among honours.

Times have changed, and there are many changes about which I'm not too happy. But it isn't all bad. Plant geneticists have improved plant strains so profoundly that gardeners in my hometown are now able to grow tomatoes and corn as well as a great many other vegetables of which my mother and I had never heard. I don't grow vegetables now the way I was taught to, and I don't grow the same standard varieties of vegetables my mother did — I garden in a smaller lot, and my tastes have become slightly more sophisticated. But I still grow vegetables with the same pleasure I felt as a child.

□   WHY GROW YOUR OWN
            VEGETABLES?

You don't really save money by growing your own vegetables. If you discount the initial cost of building up your soil and if you don't put a dollar figure on your labour, you might be able to say you're breaking even. But the truth is that value can't always be determined by a balance sheet, even though conventional economists and most of our shortsighted governments don't see it this way. There are reasons to grow at least a few vegetables of your own, and they are convincing reasons.

Homegrown vegetables almost always taste better than the ones you buy, and it isn't just pride at having grown them yourself that gives them their superior flavour. The chemical composition of many vegetables alters soon after picking. In some vegetables, sugars turn to starch, while others suffer vitamin losses and other subtle alterations. Anyone who has eaten peas, carrots or corn picked fresh from the garden understands this perfectly. And in pickling and preserving, using freshly picked vegetables sharply reduces the danger of spoilage and considerably improves the flavour.

Support often comes in strange guises: these pole beans make their way up a teepee-shaped trellis, while the tomatoes beside them are individually staked and caged. Every square inch of the bed in front, meanwhile, has been densely planted with perennials and annuals.

If you're concerned about the pesticides your body is taking in, home-grown vegetables probably contain lower levels of pesticide residue, even if you have sprayed them. If nothing else, you know what you've put on them—something you can't control with store-bought produce.

It's also worth noting that growing vegetables is an excellent teaching device for children—and for adults, come to think of it. We live in a world in which we mostly do not know where the things we use or eat daily come from. That lack of knowledge is quickly becoming a lethal luxury.

I could go on about the aesthetic rewards of growing your own vegetables. But instead, I'll turn to more practical matters: what vegetables are best for a small garden and how to grow them.

□   CROP SELECTION

This is where things get interesting for the scientist in me. A small-lot gardener must use garden space intelligently and carefully. One method is to choose vegetables that are either unavailable in stores or expensive to buy. The second is to plant space-efficient crops—vegetables that provide high yields relative to the space they take up. A third is to use your garden's vertical space to its best advantage.

A quick survey at the nearest supermarket or greengrocer will tell you which vegetables are the most costly and which specialty vegetables are not readily available. For instance, garlic and shallots are much more expensive than onions, and red onions are more expensive than cooking onions. Some supermarkets carry fresh herbs, but they are also expensive, and the selection is erratic. Worse, the dried herbs you'll find there are often about the same age as you are. On a different scale, potatoes are cheaper than carrots and beans. Logically, then, if you have to make choices, you should grow garlic and shallots and red onions instead of cooking onions. While herbs are great

to have in the garden and aesthetically pleasing to grow, you should think carefully about whether you want to bother to grow things like potatoes, cabbages and turnips. None of the latter can be stored in the freezer, and storing small crops takes a lot of effort, possibly more than it is worth.

People have their own individual likes and dislikes, and what you really like should be your ultimate garden guide, even if that means only potatoes or rutabagas. But beyond that, logic should prevail.

□   USING SPACE EFFICIENTLY

Any crop that will grow upward on a trellis, fence or other vertical support will help you use limited space more efficiently. The following are examples:
□ *Vine crops*: Winter squashes, pumpkins and melons are big plants, but they can be handled extremely efficiently in a small garden. I train my squashes and pumpkins along the fence or through my small corn patch and thence over to the fence. If you can get them up onto the roof of a garage or carport, they will do well, especially if the roof is flat. I habitually plant eating cucumbers so that they will grow vertically. The Japanese and English varieties seem to take best to this practice, although I've had success training pickling cukes onto a sloped triple tier of trellises. It makes them easier to spot and to pick, and I get double or triple the yield I would if the vines were allowed to spread along the ground.
□ *Pole beans*: Tailor-made for the compact garden, pole beans will provide far larger yields than bush beans, and they seem less vulnerable to disease and insect attack, probably because they are farther from the ground. Some of the most flavourful snap bean varieties are climbers, so there is no loss in quality. Pole beans will grow on fences and a variety of trellises and poles. I've found that tripods made out of 2-by-2s work best, although I'm not sure why. The plants seem to have difficulty climbing

poles set in an absolutely vertical position. Make sure your poles are at least 7 feet high (which means they should be at least 8½ feet long when you start), because all pole beans are vigorous plants. Scarlet runner beans are attractive enough that many gardeners grow them for floral value alone, and they are by far the most robust among the pole beans. If they had appropriate supporting structures, they would climb to 20 feet. Above about 8 feet, however, it is difficult to get at them, and you may not want to keep a helicopter in the backyard for harvesting your crop.

□ *Peas*: 'Tall Telephone' peas, snow peas and the recently developed 'Sugar Snap' pole varieties are all vigorous climbers, easily reaching six or seven feet. 'Tall Telephone' takes a little longer to mature than do bush varieties, and it dislikes early-season chills. But the peas are the equal of any in fla-

vour, the plant seems a little more tolerant of summer heat than most varieties, and it will produce double the yield of any bush pea.

□ *Tomatoes*: Depending on the degree of heat they receive, properly staked tomatoes can grow to a surprising height. Each plant has several miles of microscopic roots, and if your soil is very deep and well prepared and you do not disturb the roots, you can squeeze more plants into a smaller bed. But be careful, because if you squeeze them in too tightly, they'll produce less. Most gardening books recommend 24-inch spacing between plants, but I've planted beefsteak tomatoes 12 to 18 inches apart with no apparent loss of production.

□   TALKING TO YOUR
                              NEIGHBOURS

I may sound like a broken record about this, but the message is so important

These borderless raised beds allow for concentrated plantings of flowers, herbs and vegetables. Not only can you achieve continuous planting, but the beds themselves can be reshaped and resized from year to year, allowing for crop rotation and a refreshing new face on your garden.

LOCAL CONDITIONS

One reliable way of finding out what will grow well in your vegetable garden is to take regular walks around the neighbourhood. When I first moved into my present house, I made a point of wandering around the alleys within a two-block radius to see what people were growing. The first time I ventured out, I must have seen half a dozen strange crops and at least twice as many novel ways of growing familiar ones. I still prowl the alleys regularly, and it's a rare walk that doesn't fetch me at least one or two ideas. After you've done it several times, you'll probably find yourself focusing on certain gardens for information, ones that are either unusual or exceptionally well tended. Both the gardens and their gardeners can tell you what the best local planting dates are, which vegetables thrive in your area and how to plant them.

that I can't help repeating it: I have learned more about compact gardening from my neighbours than from any other single source. I have also received a lot of free vegetables and seed as a result, and I've been able to trade off most of my nonstorable excess.

Free vegetables are nice, but the free information and seeds are even more valuable. Ours is a professionalized civilization that needs a sense of community and ground-level empiricism more than it needs trade and commerce — which are, to my mind, mostly voodoo. Too many city people nowadays spend too much of their time socializing with television sets, traffic lights and bank machines and too little time talking to their neighbours. Neighbourhoods are an extremely sophisticated cybernetic system, and if we're not to become complete slaves to our cold, efficient technologies, we should start taking advantage of our neighbours' expertise and, in return, letting them use what we know.

As for ground-level empiricism, most gardeners sooner or later turn into amateur plant geneticists. I've been working on my own strain of scarlet runner seeds for about 13 years now, and they grow notably stronger plants than the available commercial seeds do. I don't live in an area where seed production is carried out commercially, but several people I know in the neighbourhood actively save and improve seeds. Most people who do this are happy to give them away and even happier to trade. I mentioned earlier that I obtained several exotic eastern European pole bean seeds from my neighbour Karla across the alley. One of them is an unknown but wonderful green bean that, astonishingly enough, improves the longer it stays on the vine and is in choice condition for a period of at least three weeks. From my neighbour a few doors down, I've obtained broad bean seed that grows plants just as flavourful as and far more vigorous than the English cultivars commonly available. Flower seeds and bedding plants are other

media of neighbourhood exchange among active gardeners.

Cooperation is a good idea in other gardening practices too. If your next-door neighbour is a vegetable gardener, check with him or her to make sure that the crops you intend to grow beside each other are compatible in both their biochemistry and their sunlight requirements. My next-door neighbours and I have learned to grow our peas side by side. They grow 'Sugar Snap' peas, and I grow mostly 'Tall Telephone,' but they seem to do well together and don't block each other's light. Carrots or some other low-growing crop planted next to the fence would not do as well, since the neighbouring peas would block the afternoon sun.

Biochemical compatibility is a subject I strongly suspect has as much to do with mystical conjecture as with fact. Although a lot is made of it, I have never seen any evidence that companion planting of different plant species has any positive effect. Altruism in the botanical kingdom is rare, because it is the genetic mission of nearly every plant to crowd out and defeat other plants. While I'm willing to agree that a few plants — say, corn, beans and vine squashes — like one another and that it doesn't hurt to plant them together as a space-saving measure, quite a few related species ought to be kept apart. Dill, for instance, doesn't seem to do very well around carrots, and the two relatives ought to be kept clear of one another. I like to keep beets away from spinach because they share the same pests. Separating particular species is sometimes hard to orchestrate in a small garden, and the effects of attempting it may vary from garden to garden, depending on soil conditions and the number of insect pests there seem to be in your vicinity. If pests are a problem no matter where you put your plants, you might want to have related but relatively compatible crops together — spinach and beets, for example, but not carrots and dill — so that you can limit the list of pest-control techniques to a single zone.

◻   *CROP ROTATION*

Most experts agree that vegetable crops should be rotated on at least a four-year cycle, and I try to abide by this rule whenever it is practical. In a small garden, however, it can be difficult because of the variation in light from one spot to another and the relative heights of different plants. If you find that members of the cole family—cabbages, broccoli, Brussels sprouts and cauliflower—suffer from clubroot, you may want to remove them all from the garden for at least four years. That's what I've had to do, and although I dearly love cauliflower, it hasn't been a great loss. Coles are finicky critters under the best of conditions in a small garden, and the bugs absolutely love them. They take up a lot of space for their yield, and I detect less difference in flavour between store-bought coles and homegrown ones than I do with most other vegetables.

For about five years in succession, I kept my tomatoes in the same bed because the spot I had for them was ideal —sheltered yet sunny. Instead of rotating my tomatoes to avoid diseases, I rotated the soil. Yes, it was a lot of work. But it kept me in shape, and it kept the soil in even better shape. When a shade tree I had planted nearby began to cut down on the hours of sunlight my tomato plot received, I returned to rotating my tomatoes with the rest of the vegetables.

Working in confined spaces sometimes calls for unorthodox methods. The mother of one of my friends has been growing tomatoes in precisely the same spot for 30 years without ever encountering problems with diseases. She is an assiduous and extremely meticulous composter, however, and that is almost certainly her secret. Vegetable gardening is like that: you can apply prescribed procedures with flexibility, and you can often ignore them—at least until you run afoul of whatever it is they're meant to accomplish. In a small garden, flexibility is the only rule you shouldn't break.

◻   *A CHECKLIST OF VEGETABLES*

For the most part, what you need to know about growing specific vegetables can be found on the back of the seed packages or, if you're buying seedlings, by talking to a knowledgeable person at your local garden shop. I see no point in repeating those directions. Instead, I'll talk about the best ways to grow vegetables in a garden of limited size, and I'll throw in any tricks I've learned for making them perform better. I should say at the outset that growing vegetables requires a degree of vigilance and perseverance not demanded by experimentation with annuals or a few standard perennials. You've got to be there at the beginning, the middle and the end, or you'll be wasting your time —and wasting food. You'll have to weed, you'll have to cultivate, and you'll have to be available for midwife

duty when the time is right. If you're not there when the harvest is ready, you'll be missing out on one of gardening's greatest pleasures.

◻   *Artichokes*

There are two distinct kinds of artichokes: globe artichokes—the green ones rich folks like to eat—and Jerusalem artichokes, which look, act and taste something like potatoes. Surprisingly, neither is very difficult to grow. Globe artichokes are a relative of the common thistle. They're easily germinated indoors, and in warmer climates, they can sometimes last through the winter to regenerate again and again on the same stalk. But unless you have perfect light conditions and live in a hot climate, they're not very productive. And they take up a lot of space. Every

READING SEEDS

You've probably read those cryptic bracketed messages—the ones that say "86 days" or "120 days" or "43 days"—printed in seed catalogues and on seed packages, and you've probably wondered exactly what they meant. Well, the truth is that they don't mean anything very exact. It's most unlikely that a tomato-seed packet that says "76 days" inside the brackets contains seed that will produce tomatoes in exactly that time. So when you read those numbers, don't take it personally if they don't turn out to be precise. They are guidelines, and taken with a grain of salt, they can be helpful. Early tomatoes, for instance, do produce before the beefsteaks, and 70-day corn will be ready a week or two earlier than an 80-day variety. Remember, though, that there are such factors to take into account as average temperatures in your area, how cool the evenings become and how good your soil is.

few years, just for the fun of it, I grow them in the flowerbed and let them go past the edible stage to flower. The blossoms are quite spectacular, and they're a good conversation piece.

Jerusalem artichokes, while similar to potatoes, are to my mind inferior in flavour. They're fine in stews, but you have to be very careful, or they'll boil down to a tasteless gruel. I grew them for a couple of years and then gave up.

□   *Beans*

As I've said, I prefer the pole varieties because their climbing ability makes them so much more space-efficient and thus appropriate for a compact garden. I plant beans at least a week later than tomatoes—they seem to dislike cool nights when they're germinating. If you don't get early frosts, staggering your plantings is a good idea. I've done this with 'Blue Lake' beans, as have several of my neighbours. The late-producing varieties seem to be better flavoured, as well as more prolific. Even though they're called pole beans, they don't really like climbing vertical poles, particularly if the poles are thick. Vertical wire or rope seems to be fine, as are poles set in tripods so that they have a slight angle. Weed but don't cultivate around the roots of beans—they don't appreciate it at all. If your season is short or uncertain, stick with bush varieties. They're reliable and tasty.

□ *Fava (broad) beans*: With a flavour remotely resembling that of limas, fava beans don't look or act like any other beans. I happen to be nuts about them. Their flavour is unique, and they're worth growing just for the fun of shelling them (you eat the seeds and discard the velvet-lined pod). Favas can be part of your first planting, and they don't like warm weather, which can make them taste bitter. They are not vines, but they do grow from three to six feet tall and seem to appreciate some support when the flowers set. Aphids adore them, but a fine spray with the hose or a hand sprayer loaded with in-

secticidal soap will remove the little beasties. Insect attacks scar the pods but don't seem to affect the flavour. Europeans often let favas ripen on the plant and harvest them as a dry shell bean. I prefer them fresh—boiled and slathered with butter. If you like them this way, make sure you harvest the pods while they're young.

□ *Green beans*: I can't think of a green bean that is equal in quality or flavour to 'Blue Lake,' although the bush varieties have some pretty exotic specimens. As noted, the pole varieties are more disease-free and far more prolific. Scarlet runner, 'Kentucky Wonder,' 'Romano,' 'Blue Lake' and even pinto make good snap beans, and pinto and 'Romano' are excellent shell beans. Scarlet runner beans have attractive scarlet blossoms, but be sure to pick the pods while they're very young (less than six inches) because they quickly become too stringy to eat.

□ *Wax beans*: I prefer these yellow beans to green beans because of their flavour, but until recently, I didn't grow them much because I thought they were exclusively a bush bean. A few years ago, however, my neighbour Karla gave me some seeds that turned out to produce exquisite yellow pole beans. They're very prolific, and I leave extras on the vine to dry as shell beans. I'd tell you the variety if I knew it, but as hard as I've looked, I haven't been able to find them anywhere. Several other pole wax beans have come on the market in the last few years. I've tried them but have not been impressed with either their vigour or their flavour.

□   *Beets*

The soil for beets should be relatively light, free of rocks and well limed. Beets are a cool-weather crop, and like carrots, they positively despise manure unless it has been thoroughly composted and integrated into the soil. Both beets and carrots seem to have trouble getting their roots through manure. The carrots get hairy and turn into odd shapes; beets just sit there pretending that they're colourful spinach plants.

I plant beets in rows about four to five inches apart and cultivate carefully with a hand cultivator. Since beets also like to be rotated, they can be problematic in a small garden. I grow them for pickling and because young beets cooked with their greens are a culinary delight. The roots seem to be impervious to disease, but the leaves are susceptible to leaf miners and leaf spot. If you see leaf miners in your beets, spray with diazinon as soon as possible, because otherwise they'll go after other leafy crops too, particularly spinach. Don't eat the sprayed greens. Leaf spot can be controlled with a fungicide if necessary. 'Detroit Dark Red' is a faithful producer, and I'm fond of 'Cylindra,' which seems to provide better yields in cramped quarters. In the past several years, I've planted fewer conventional varieties because my father grows them in bulk and is happy to give me all I need. I use the space I reserve for beets for a white variety from the British company Thompson & Morgan. I've developed a powerful liking for beets in stews, and with the white ones, the stew doesn't look as if you've cut off your thumb or dismembered one of your enemies and tossed the parts in just before serving.

□   *Broccoli*

In my opinion, broccoli is not a prime crop for a small garden, but it can be a good producer if you're lucky enough to avoid diseases. I recommend more disease-resistant and prolific Chinese varieties, even though they aren't quite as pretty as some of the others. The trick with any broccoli is to cut the heads soon after they form and to prevent succeeding shoots from flowering. Broccoli, in common with most of its relatives, likes soil with a pH slightly above 7, and the high pH helps to avoid the clubroot, blackleg and black rot to which it is susceptible (nice, picturesque names for plant diseases, no?).

If your broccoli contracts any of these, pull the plants out, do not compost them, and do not plant broccoli or any of its relatives in that spot for at least four years. It sounds drastic, but the diseases are at least as disgusting as they sound, particularly clubroot.

□   *Brussels Sprouts*

These frost lovers share the same problems as broccoli and should be treated in roughly the same way. In addition, cabbageworms adore Brussels sprouts. The worms are best controlled biologically, either by spraying the plants with *Bacillus thuringiensis* or by tearing out your hair. When I had Brussels sprouts in the garden, I planted them later than broccoli or cabbage. They can take some frost—it really improves their flavour. 'Jade Cross Hybrid' and 'Long Island Improved' are prime strains.

□   *Cabbage*

Treat cabbages as if they were Brussels sprouts. Slightly heavier feeders, they are also prime targets for cabbageworms although slightly less susceptible to clubroot and its loathsome kin. Red cabbage gives better value for space, but it is just a touch harder to grow. Preferred cultivars are 'Meteor,' 'King Cole' and 'Savoy King' for green cabbage and 'Red Danish' for red.

□   *Carrots*

Carrots need generous helpings of water when they are germinating and when they are little. I plant them in wide rows about six inches apart in soil I have lightened by generous additions of deeply dug builder's sand. In the last few years, I've gone to permanent beds for my carrots, mainly because they have only one real enemy: the carrot rust fly larva. I plant carrot seed with a sprinkling of 5 percent diazinon granules and then douse them later in the season with a liquid solution of diazinon, usually in early August when the second generation of carrot rust fly larvae is on the prowl.

A space-efficient crop with a built-in bonus: the flowers of these scarlet runner beans are beautiful and plentiful, and the plant flourishes when staked properly.

True villains, carrot rust flies will destroy your entire crop if they are not controlled. They usually lay their eggs twice a year, once early and once late in the season. Make an effort to find out what the dates for those festivities are in your area by asking your neighbours or the staff at the garden centre, because that's the time to apply the diazinon, which breaks down swiftly in the soil. If you apply it too early or too late, you'll have wasted your time.

Carrot seeds are small and slow to germinate, so I plant radish seeds along with them and take a crop of fast-growing radishes from the same bed. If your soil is heavy, plant cultivars like 'Nantes Half Long' or 'Amsterdam Forcing.' If you have light, sandy soil, plant the long varieties. The small gourmet cultivars are as tasty as advertised and are sensible choices for a very small garden

or if you have kids, who seem to like miniature vegetables.

☐ *Cauliflower*

I love cauliflower, but it's undoubtedly the hardest brassica to grow. If your soil is good and you are a patient person, go for it—with the aid of a good manual and some tranquillizers.

There are some really silly-looking cauliflowers around these days, with purple or brilliant green heads, and one called 'Romanesque' that looks like the result of Salvador Dali's spending some time in a genetics lab trying to cross broccoli with cauliflower. I grew some, and it tasted fine, although I wasn't quite sure what I was eating. Growing these new designer cauliflowers will probably make you even crazier than growing the conventional kinds. And your sensible friends won't want to eat such strangely coloured vegetables, par-

ticularly if you serve them with cheese sauce, which is how good cooks always serve cauliflower.

☐ *Corn*

These tall plants take up a lot of space, but fresh corn is so delicious that I grow it anyway. Corn is best grown in a block. It doesn't matter if the block consists of 9 plants or 90, you won't get much unless you stroke the pollen onto the silk of the individual ears by hand when the tassels flower. If you don't do this, you'll get empty or near-empty ears.

Corn is an extremely heavy feeder, so make sure your soil is well supplied with humus and fertilizer before planting. When the plants are about 18 inches high, a sidedressing of compost mixed with a high-nitrogen fertilizer is almost a necessity. Harvest the corn young, as soon as the silk turns brown, and cook immediately—no, instantly.

The geraniums tucked in among the

lettuce will continue to flower long after

the lettuce has been harvested.

Meanwhile, the bush beans, onions and

squash thrive in these wide raised beds.

The sugar in corn rapidly turns to starch after picking, and the difference between truly fresh-picked corn and store-bought corn is astonishing. I'm a fan of the 'Eleni' family of sweet corn and have grown it successfully in a number of different locales. But check carefully to see which cultivars do best in your climate. Some corn varieties will mature in a remarkably short time, and some do better in hot climates than others. You can obtain seed for white corn, yellow corn, white and yellow mixed on each ear, decorative Indian corn and even blue corn.

☐ *Cucumbers*

Cucumbers will grow pretty well anywhere. Heavy feeders that particularly like composted manure, probably for the nitrogen, they seem to be a little more sensitive to poor drainage and cold soil than most vegetables. (Tips on growing cucumbers can be found on page 49.) I grow the Japanese and English varieties for eating because the peel isn't bitter, but 'Straight Eight' is a reliable and less fragile standby, as is 'National Pickling' for making dills and other pickles. Using fresh garden dill and pickling cukes no more than four hours out of the garden guarantees dill pickles that won't spoil.

☐ *Garlic*

Normally considered either a herb or a member of the onion family, garlic, to my mind, occupies its own distinct category as both herb and vegetable — and an indispensable one at that. I use it in salads, in pasta dishes and with fish and meat (I have a delicious chicken recipe that calls for 26 cloves). In early summer, one of my favourite treats is whole fresh garlic cloves dipped in olive oil, salt and pepper, then wrapped in tinfoil and tossed on the barbecue. I even pickle garlic.

Not surprisingly, my procedure for planting garlic is fairly complicated. The first thing I do is locate the freshest large-cloved garlic available in the mar-ket or supermarket. Before I buy it, I pick apart a clove to find out how fresh it is and whether the cloves are large enough. I've never encountered any evidence to suggest that garlic is treated by commercial producers to prevent it from sprouting, so buying your seed garlic in the supermarket is much cheaper than buying it from a nursery.

Some experts claim that garlic does not like particularly rich soil, but I have never seen the logic of that. I plant the separated cloves in rich, deeply dug, fertilized soil. After raking the soil smooth and picking out any rocks I can find, I punch a pattern of two-to-three-inch-deep holes into the soil surface with a piece of ¾-inch dowling and drop the cloves in, pointed end up, then rake the soil back over them. I plant most of my garlic in the fall, mainly because the garlic available in the stores is fresher then, but garlic planted in the very early spring seems to do about as well. Harvesting garlic is quite simple. When the stems begin to feel a bit loose if pressed between your finger and thumb, they are ready. I find this a slightly more accurate measure than waiting until the foliage begins to turn yellow.

I have yet to find an insect that attacks garlic with any real enthusiasm, and crops grown in its near vicinity also seem to be freer of pests than they normally are. I won't go into the usual litany about the wonders of garlic, although I agree that most of the claims made for it are accurate, particularly the culinary ones. I think many of the claims for its medicinal properties may be a little optimistic. If you eat enough of it on a regular enough basis, however, it probably does work as a very mild antibiotic. It wards off vampires for pretty much the same reasons.

I try to plant as much garlic as I can — as much as 100 square feet. That may seem like a lot for a small garden, but I don't plant it in a single block. I put garlic in wherever a moderately sunny space is available. It keeps well if sun-dried in braids and stored in a dark,

cool spot, and six-to-eight-clove braids make excellent gifts.

☐ *Lettuce*

For a number of reasons, lettuce is a good crop for small gardens. It grows quickly and, in many areas, can be grown throughout the season, even though it is not a heat lover and most varieties tend to bolt in hot weather. The secret of growing lettuce is to plant the seeds fairly thickly and then pick and eat the thinnings as the plants grow. In most areas, by planting only a few feet of row lettuce every two weeks (and by beginning the season with seedlings started indoors), it is possible to have lettuce from the last spring frost through to the first frosts in the fall.

Lettuce has four distinct varieties. Head, or iceberg, lettuce, which until recently was just about the only lettuce commercially grown in North America, is in my opinion unfit for human consumption. Butterhead lettuce is easy to grow and is much more palatable than its tight-headed relative, although it becomes bitter with the slightest heat and will bolt. Even so, garden-grown lettuce of any variety has more flavour than commercial lettuce. Romaine, or cos, lettuce is a hardy all-

purpose lettuce often used by Europeans as a cooked vegetable. There is a wide variety of looseleaf lettuces. 'Oak Leaf' is more tolerant of heat than the others, and 'Winter Density' will take you later into the fall.

Some relatives of lettuce can both lengthen the season and provide some magic in the kitchen. Endive is more tolerant of both cold and heat. It has a sharper flavour than lettuce and needs to be either grown in shade or blanched, or it will be bitter. Corn salad is a flavoursome cool-weather substitute and, in some climates, can be wintered over for salad greens in the very early spring.

Slugs really like young lettuce plants, and so do most night-feeding caterpillars. Many gardening books recommend spraying lettuce when insects attack, but I make a practice of not spraying any lettuce crop. Life is just too short—mine and the lettuce's when it is best to eat.

☐ *Melons*

Like their relatives the squashes, melons are actually fruits. They need three months of warm nights and hot days to mature, so for any northerly locale, they are a marginal crop, even if seedlings are started indoors, carefully nurtured and kept from cold conditions after planting. The least weather-fragile short-season variety is the cantaloupe, but just about every year, plant geneticists come up with a new cultivar adapted to shorter growing seasons and cooler weather. My Chinese neighbours grow an Oriental variety of melon without too much difficulty by mulching with a combination of cardboard and plastic. As a northerner, I grew up without melons, and it is one of the few garden denizens for which I haven't developed much of a taste. Perhaps that's because the first time I encountered them, at the age of about 7, I somehow got the idea that they were called melvins. My worst enemy was a boy named Melvin, and I've never

Convenience should always be a consideration in a small space. This gardener has planted the lettuce garden —including romaine, oak-leaf, red-leaf and Boston lettuce at various stages of maturity—just outside the back door for easy kitchen access, while neighbouring beds include shrubs and flowers.

ON ONIONS

If you live in an area where cool, rainy weather is a frequent occurrence around midsummer, you may find that your onion sets form seed heads instead of plumping out as they should. Without getting too complicated about it, I should tell you that onions are really annuals, and extended periods of cool weather—between 48 and 60 degrees F—trigger a genetic signal that tells them their life is about over and it is time to reproduce. There are three things you can do about this problem if you have it every year. The first is to rely on onions that you grow from seed. The second is to drop six-mil plastic tents over your onions when the cool, wet weather hits. The tents will raise the temperature enough to block the genetic signals. The third thing you can do is what I do most of the time—hope for warmer weather, pop off the seed heads as soon as they start to appear and live with the smaller onions. Don't store onions that have formed seed heads, because they don't keep.

been fond of Melvins or melons since.

Like the squashes, melons are best grown in compost-loaded mounds, and they like to be fed with a chemical dressing (20-20-20) when the vines are established and again later as they are setting fruit. Pick off any fruit that sets after about mid-August. Early-maturing melon varieties are 'Burpee Hybrid' (72 days) and 'You Sweet Thing' (70 days), which is a watermelon. A particularly suicidal variety is 'Golden Beauty' (120 days), a white-fleshed casaba. Except in my imagination, there is no known cultivar called 'Melvin.'

□   *Onions*

Onions are among the most gratifying crops to grow, and one can easily achieve success with some varieties simply through proper bed preparation, watering and weeding. One of the real pleasures of vegetable gardening, for both the eye and the nose, lies in harvesting members of the onion family.

For some reason I've not deciphered, expert opinion on how best to grow the various kinds of onions varies more than for any other garden vegetable. I find that onions seem to like a slightly sandy soil, rich but not too rich in humus and nutrient-weighted toward phosphorus. I feed mine with bulb food (3-15-6) at least once during the growing season, although I've been known to run out to the garden late at night to toss a handful of 6-8-6 into the onion patch for the purely neurotic reason that I can't see the bulbs actually growing. I plant quite a variety of onions, and over the years, I've developed some fairly idiosyncratic approaches toward them that I'll pass on to you. The first is that I try to base my plantings on two criteria: crop value and utility.

□ *Shallots*: The most expensive onions to buy are shallots, although for the life of me, I don't know why: they're no harder to grow than any other onion, they keep extraordinarily well, and their utility in the kitchen is hard to overestimate. Quite simply, they make

any sauce that calls for onions at least 40 percent better than conventional onions do. As early in the spring as the soil can be worked, I go down to the local market, pick out the largest European or California shallots I can find and plant the separated cloves on six-inch centres. They seem quite susceptible to root maggot attacks, so I work some granular 5 percent diazinon into the soil as I'm planting them. They mature a little sooner than most onions do—in my area, usually a shade after midsummer. I braid and sun-dry them for a week and then hang the braids in the basement. Last year, one braid fell into a cardboard box, and when I discovered it there 14 months later, the bulbs were still in prime condition.

□ *Bulb onions*: I grow several varieties of bulb onions, some of which I start from seed indoors and some from store-bought sets, which are juvenile bulbs grown commercially from seed and harvested before they discover sex, drugs and rock 'n' roll. Onions from sets are easier to grow than those from seed, and in most communities, the sweeter red and Spanish onions are now available as sets, along with the familiar yellow sets. Whether you're growing from seed or using sets, it's a good idea to share with your neighbours, because you'll wind up with more of any single variety than you can possibly use in a small garden. Plant sets early and shallowly on three-inch centres, and keep the patch carefully weeded. I don't cultivate onions because I grow them in grid patterns and plant them generally closer together than most gardeners do. They have very shallow roots that are easily disturbed. If and when the tops start to yellow, break them gently at the top of the bulb. 'Southport Red Globe,' 'White Sweet Spanish' and 'Silver Queen' (pickling) are all nonkeepers that are pleasant to have, and 'Autumn Spice' is an excellent keeper. 'Spartan Sleeper' takes longer to mature but, as a bonus, stores even better. I sun-dry my onions on the porch in partial sun for about 10 days before storing, turning them daily.

□ *Bunching onions (scallions):* Most of these are really shallots and should be planted sparsely. If you use a lot of green onions, try planting one or two sets at a time throughout the season. That will ensure a steady but adequate supply. If you live in a mild climate, you might do what I've done, which is to plant perennial green onions in your herb or perennial bed. 'Tokyo White Bunching' is a hardy cultivar. Its flavour isn't quite up to that of the annual varieties, but it's adequate for most cooking uses and, in my climate at least, available year-round.

□ *Chives:* Everybody needs this mild onion relative for garnishes and salads. Chives are easy to grow and don't seem to need or even like terribly rich soil. I have three clumps of them in my herb garden, one of which I cut regularly. I leave the other two to flower. If allowed to flower, they can be very pretty plants, and they don't mind shade, unlike other members of the family. Garlic chives, which taste like their name, also do well in the herb bed. Late in the season, they also flower and are extremely attractive. The trick to cutting chives, incidentally, is not to do it as if you're giving the plant a haircut but to cut a narrow section right back to within an inch of the roots and let it regenerate.

□ *Leeks:* I have a special fondness for leeks. I like their mild flavour, and I like the fact that they let me do some double cropping. I start them outdoors in a makeshift cold frame in very early spring, then transplant them into the garden bed when they're about pencil size. Because my fall-planted garlic is ready for harvesting in late June or early July, I redig the garlic beds immediately and transplant the pencil-sized leeks into it, using a piece of ¾-inch dowling to punch four-to-five-inch-deep holes on three-inch centres. I drop the leeks into the holes and sprinkle generously with water. The entire operation usually takes about two hours.

In the fall, the garlic moves on to a new spot in the garden, where it does its job of disinfecting the soil. Neat, eh? If your vegetable garden is small or if your winter frosts are too severe, you won't be able to do this, but I still think leeks are a worthwhile crop. They are excellent for using garden space after midsummer, they seem to be pest- and disease-free, and their flavour improves considerably after the first frosts. Even in cold climates, they can be dug up to midwinter if carefully mulched.

□ *Parsnips*

Near relatives of carrots, parsnips require similar conditions and suffer from the same pests. Experts recommend that carrots and parsnips not be grown near one another, but that kind of advice is easier to follow in Rolling Acres than in a small garden. If you like parsnips, they are a worthwhile crop to grow. They winter even better than carrots and can be planted later for harvest in the fall (and even in winter, if your climate allows it). Their pattern of growth is different from that of carrots: they are only choice when mature. (You don't hear about people eating baby parsnips, do you?) 'Hollow Crown' is a standby (with a misleading name), and 'All America' is a variety that matures a little earlier. Normal children absolutely hate parsnips, and so do neighbours. You should plant them only if you really love them and not with the expectation that they will make you popular at parties.

□ *Peas*

I've already made my case for tall varieties of peas (page 50), so I won't repeat myself. No matter what variety you choose, peas take up a lot of space, so deciding to plant them is a judgement call that has more to do with culinary aesthetics than economics. They're heavy feeders, but they're also the kind of plants that return nitrogen to the soil. I plant them in slightly raised double rows a little more thickly than is

□   □   □   □   □

POTATO PRIMER

If you have your heart set on growing potatoes, prepare a special sunny bed, which you can condition with 6-8-6 and peat moss (which provides acidic humus), and hope for the best. Don't use store-bought potatoes for seed, because most potatoes have been treated to prevent premature sprouting. Seed potatoes from the garden centre come in rather large quantities and are quite expensive, so you might try sprouting potatoes from your local organic-food store. (It's a good test of how organic the establishment really is.) Make sure you're clear on which variety you're planting. Early and late potatoes have quite distinct maturing patterns. 'Norland' is a good late cultivar; 'White Rose' is an early variety. 'Yukon Gold' sits somewhere in between and is more tolerant of problem conditions than most of the other varieties, but it won't keep well. In a small garden, you don't really want to grow enough potatoes for storing anyway.

usually recommended and mound an inch or two more of soil or mature compost around the roots when the plants reach six or eight inches in height. Support netting of various kinds is available in garden stores, but my Chinese neighbours use tall twigs and string, and I think the twigs do a better job than netting. Peas need more moisture than other vegetables, and bathing the whole row with the hose daily, top to bottom, helps them get it. Try to eat peas within minutes of picking, and keep the vines picked, because the sugars quickly turn to starches if they are left too long. Pick the edible-podded varieties ('Sugar Snap') as the pods are just beginning to fill. Sow early, and then at two-week intervals until early summer. They don't particularly like hot weather, so don't go much beyond that.

Cold, wet weather in early spring can produce powdery mildew, a problem that can be controlled with sulphur, Dinocap or devout prayer. Pea mosaic, which is aphid-borne, can't be controlled except by keeping aphids off the peas. I try to plant my fava beans near the peas, because the aphids like the favas much better and usually ignore the peas if they're given the choice. If you have a long growing season, redig the soil when your early peas are finished and plant lettuce or radishes.

◻   *Peppers*

You need lots of heat and a long season to grow peppers successfully. They don't seem to require much more than that, since they're not heavy feeders and most bugs don't like them. But if your summers aren't long and hot, they are a marginal crop, as is their relative the eggplant. Sweet peppers are easier, mainly because they can be harvested at any stage of growth. The hot peppers — a startling number of different kinds exist — must be left to mature on the plants. If your late-summer nights get cold, shelter peppers with six-mil plastic tents and hope for the best. A sweet green pepper called 'Ace Hybrid' is the best bet for cooler climates.

◻   *Potatoes*

I'll make this really simple: don't grow potatoes in a small garden. They take up a great deal of space and are generally incompatible with other crops because of the soil acidity they need in order to thrive. About 3,000 things can go wrong with potatoes, most of them related to soil conditions. Too much humus produces bony potatoes, and a high pH and manure cause scab. And not surprisingly, potato beetles like potatoes, as do most other garden pests.

If you must grow potatoes, go after some of the exotic varieties, like those yellow European banana potatoes you sometimes see in gourmet grocery stores. They're flavourful, and they take up less space than conventional varieties. You'll have to sprout them yourself, since I've never seen seed potatoes for this variety.

Sweet potatoes and yams are even harder to grow, requiring about four months of really warm weather to produce a crop. If your season is cool or short, forget about them, however much you like their flavour.

◻   *Radishes*

Radishes grow very quickly and dislike heat. I plant them with carrots and along the edges of my pickling-cucumber beds, where they will be picked and finished before the others can get into gear. I also plant them late in the summer when the nights are getting cool.

Root maggots and wireworms adore radishes, so radish seeds absolutely must be planted with 5 percent granular diazinon. If you object to using pesticides, don't even try to grow radishes. In my experience, all you'll get are the maggots. I have a fondness for 'French Breakfast' radishes (with butter, French bread and a cup of coffee), and 'Cherry Belle' also has an excellent flavour. If you like white radishes, 'White Icicle' is a mild later variety. 'Celestial' is a good later daikon type that will grow 6 to 10 inches long. Read the package directions carefully for the later varieties, because they're tricky to work with. My experience is that daikon-type radishes do best with late-summer plantings, but that may be peculiar to my climate.

☐ *Rhubarb*

This perennial likes very deep, rich soil and dislikes being disturbed. It doesn't seem to require full sun, so if a corner of your garden has partial shade, put your rhubarb there. About every three or four years, divide the plant to keep the heavy yellow roots from becoming overcrowded. When the plant starts to produce inedible seed stalks, pick them off in order to promote a longer harvest. Fertilize each spring with a combination of 6-8-6 and compost, and pick the biggest stalks, but don't harvest more than 50 percent of them. Rhubarb is propagated from roots rather than seed. When you're starting out, try to get a piece from a neighbour who happens to be dividing his or her rhubarb. If you're going to a garden shop, look for 'MacDonald' (red stalks) or 'Victoria' (green stalks). In areas with mild winters, go for 'Cherry.' Incidentally, you can't tell if rhubarb is ready by looking at the colour of the leaves or stalks. The whole plant tells you. It ought to look full and healthy, and you should be able to see new stalks beginning to push their way out of the root crown. Rhubarb leaves don't taste like rhubarb and are mildly poisonous, so don't get any funny New Age ideas about putting them in your salads.

☐ *Spinach*

Spinach and its substitutes are uncomplicated, fast-growing crops that require nitrogen-rich soil and don't like hot weather. They should be treated in much the same fashion as lettuce, except that they are slightly more sensitive to hot weather and slightly more tolerant of cool weather. 'Melody' is a fine new variety that withstands heat better than do older varieties. 'Long-standing Bloomsdale' is also excellent.

Swiss chard and mustard greens are spinach substitutes. Swiss chard is a good choice for late-summer planting, and mustard greens, more piquant than spinach, grow more quickly and are fine in the early spring. Neither has quite the flavour of spinach, however. New Zealand spinach is a heat-tolerant substitute that is adequate for cooking but terrible as a salad green. If you have lamb's quarters, or pigweed, growing as a weed in your garden, it is at least the equal of spinach for cooking, but don't let it go to seed, because it harbours leaf miners, which can destroy spinach-type crops. 'Fordhook Giant' and the attractive 'Rhubarb Chard' are the premier chards, and 'Tendergreen' is the standard for mustard-green types.

☐ *Squash*

When I was a youngster, I was once forced to eat boiled squash and, sensible lad that I was, responded by taking a drive on the porcelain bus. For the next decade, just thinking of squash made me ill. Not anymore. Squash is not only delicious but is among the most satisfying and site-flexible plants for small gardens. There are two distinct groups, summer and winter, and each comes in both vine and bush form. Summer squashes include zucchini, scallopini, crookneck and the slightly later vegetable marrow and spaghetti squash. They're called summer squashes because they should be eaten while they're young and immature. (They really ought to be called spring squashes, but that would be confusing because the plants don't produce until at least mid-summer.) You should try to harvest zucchini and crookneck squash while they are less than six inches in length and scallopini squash less than four inches in diameter. Harvest vegetable marrow and spaghetti squash when they are just short of full size—somewhere between 9 and 12 inches—and do not allow the skins to harden.

When space is limited, sometimes the only way to go is up: this sturdy arbour supports both a morning glory and a miniature-pumpkin vine. In turn, their leaves provide shelter for shade-loving plants like the potted impatiens beneath.

Winter squashes come in an even greater variety of shapes, sizes and flavours, including pumpkins. Winter squashes should be left to mature in the garden as long as possible, preferably until just before the first frost. After the stem ends have been dipped in a mild solution of bleach, winter squash should be stored in a cool, dry spot. Some can last up to six months.

All squashes should be planted in roughly the same way as cucumbers, with a greater emphasis, if possible, on humus-rich soil. I occasionally plant them in a container of half-rotted compost, and they positively love the experience. Bedding plants can be acquired for most of the common varieties, but those aren't always the best ones. I start my special favourites indoors under growing lights in April, although I do plant some of my summer squashes directly in the garden as seed so that I can have a steady supply through the summer and early fall.

The flavours of winter squashes are quite subtle, and aficionados are often willing to start fistfights over which is best. In terms of both productivity and flavour, I think it is hard to beat the acorn (or Danish) squashes. They have a rich, slightly nutty flavour, and they keep extremely well, their flavour improving several months after harvest. The butternuts taste the way they sound. When they're at their best, they're more buttery than the acorns, but I think their flavour is a trifle bland, and they're choice for a much shorter period. Turban-type squashes look interesting and keep well, but in my opinion, their flavour is notably inferior to either the butternuts or the acorns.

'Table Queen' is a fine-flavoured vine-type acorn, while 'Table King' is the bush equivalent – equal in flavour but less prolific. 'Buttercup' is the best butternut type (a vine), while 'Sweet Mama' is the choice turban squash. 'Gold Nugget' is a golden acorn bush type that you can harvest young as summer squash. I'd stay away from the large Hubbards unless you have a big family with disabled taste buds, know some hippies who still live on squash pies and brown rice, or are considering yet another remake of *Invasion of the Body Snatchers*. Small children will enjoy growing squashes, but I ought to warn you that they'll ask you how squash got such a silly name. Sorry, I don't know the answer.

'Big Max' is a very reliable standard pumpkin for jack-o'-lanterns. For cooking and baking, 'Small Sugar' is good. Both are vigorous vines, so plan accordingly. If you live in the eastern part of the continent, you might try 'Atlantic Giant,' the variety that in the right conditions produces those 500-pound monsters that can only be moved with a forklift. I planted some once out of curiosity, and they didn't do very well. I was more relieved than disappointed: a 500-pound pumpkin would have created real problems in my backyard.

Over the years, I've found that pumpkins are slightly more fragile in the early stages than are most squashes, but that may be a local aberration. None of my more sober-minded neighbours grow pumpkins, so I'm not sure. If you're trying to grow a very large pumpkin, there are a few tricks you can employ. Wait until your plant sets a fruit in a convenient spot, prop the young fruit atop a water-filled one-gallon paint can (or equivalent), then remove all succeeding blossoms from the plant before they have a chance to set fruit. The can will elevate your pumpkin above the coolness and moisture of the soil, and the water will provide a small degree of evening heat.

I grew an 87-pound 'Big Max' a few years ago that drew raves on Halloween, but the next year, I lost one of equal size to vandals in mid-October. I hope they got hernias dragging it down the alley.

Tomatoes

For 200 years, these tropical relatives of deadly nightshade were thought to be poisonous and were grown strictly as ornamentals. But now, no one believes that tomatoes are either tropical or ornamental. In fact, they've become the most commonly grown vegetable in North American home gardens. I think of them as the rocket scientists of the vegetable patch. There is no "best" variety and no "best" way to grow tomatoes. The more years I grow tomatoes, the more I find out about them, and my methods are constantly evolving as I learn new tricks.

Most home gardeners like to grow a lot of tomatoes. I plant 10 or 12 plants every year, because whatever I don't use I can always give away to friends who don't have gardens. On occasion, I give some to my neighbours, even though most of them grow their own. I plant a range of types as well: four paste tomato plants for canning and making

WHAT'S AT STAKE

There's no great secret to staking tomatoes. It's more a matter of simple common sense. Unless I have something of comparable length and strength, I use six-foot-long, one-inch-diameter commercial stakes, placing them three inches from the plants as soon as I remove the tents. For ties, I recycle heavy plastic bags, which I cut into two-inch-wide strips. Don't use string or wire to tie your tomatoes to the stakes, because the thinness of the tie can easily strangle your plant, particularly as the ripening tomatoes put a heavier load on it.

Another tip: use bare copper wire to build support trellises for tomatoes. Although I don't know anything about the scientific basis of this technique, it seems to work, especially with cherry tomatoes. Several gardeners I know swear by it, and my own experiments corroborate their enthusiasm.

pickles, two cherry tomatoes, two early varieties for early-summer eating and two beefsteak tomatoes for later in the summer and to impress my neighbours with the big tomatoes I can grow. I also plant two new cultivars a year for experimental purposes.

I plant my tomatoes as six-inch bedding plants a little earlier than most people do. I dig a hole about a foot deep and crumple a sheet of newspaper at the bottom. The newspaper will give the young tomato roots an early supply of moisture—and something to assuage their thirst for knowledge—while they're starting off. I cover that with an inch or two of compost and bury the seedling up to its neck so that only two inches of it is above the surface. That leaves me with a four- or five-inch depression, most of which I fill in as the young tomato plant develops. This encourages the young plant, which can sprout roots from any part of the stem, to develop a much stronger and more secure root system.

Young tomatoes really dislike cool soil temperatures. Even temporary cool temperatures will cause root shock that can set them back weeks. So right after planting, I put a tent frame four or five feet tall over the entire bed and cover it with six-mil plastic. I leave the tent over the tomatoes, rain or shine, until mid-June or until the first flower clusters are formed, opening it only to water the growing seedlings, which I do with buckets of warm water, never a hose. This method usually guarantees that I have tomatoes at least two or three weeks earlier in the summer than anyone else in the neighbourhood. If your climate heats up earlier in the summer than mine does, you may want to shorten the duration of the tenting, but the basic principle remains sound wherever you are: the more heat tomato plants get while young, the more tomatoes they provide.

Tomatoes are extremely heavy feeders, requiring deeply dug, rich soil. They also require a steady—not too much, not too little—supply of moisture, and they don't like to be watered directly from the hose because they are sensitive to cold water. I keep a full-sized plastic garbage can near the tomato bed, into which I dump half a bag of steer manure and a one-eighth-strength solution of 7-28-28 chemical fertilizer. Then I fill it with the hose. The result is a supply of soupy manure tea and a steady and abundant supply of nutrients that the tea helps to put into digestible form for the tomatoes. I water the plants every second morning with this tea (every morning in very hot weather). After I've watered, I refill the half-empty garbage can with water. It'll last two weeks, then I repeat the process until the plants stop setting fruit.

Tomato plants need to be supported because ripening tomatoes become rather heavy. I generally plant staking varieties, partly because the bush varieties don't seem to do as well in my usually moist climate, but mainly because the staking varieties allow a more economical use of space in a small garden.

Choosing tomato varieties is a complicated matter. Don't believe everything you read about them. Conventional wisdom tells us, for instance, that the beefsteak varieties are the biggest, sweetest and best. That's only true if your summers are very hot and the nights warm. I live in a cool-to-moderate climate, and the summer nights don't stay as warm as they might because of the ocean breezes. I've found that the earlier, midsized tomatoes have the best flavour and that the beefsteaks tend to be a little watery. Take a hard look at your local conditions, and judge accordingly. If your climate is subject to early frosts, I'd recommend staying with the earlier varieties. If you are in a really northerly climate, plant the new subarctic varieties. They are quite tasty and will set and ripen in poor conditions with astonishing reliability. They are thus good candidates for extra-early tomatoes in any garden. Remember that the object of growing

tomatoes is to be able to eat them vine-ripened. Check to see what your neighbours have been planting.

I've grown my own tomato seedlings, but it can be tricky to produce a truly healthy seedling. Tomatoes like more heat than most other seedlings, and producing healthy ones may cost you the health of some of the others. In recent years, I've purchased most of my needs from local plant nurseries. Go to the nurseries early, when the plants come in from the commercial greenhouses they're grown in, and buy only the healthiest and largest specimens. Plant them immediately because they have just come out of a hot greenhouse.

If frosts begin to threaten before all your tomatoes have ripened, take the entire vine out — very carefully — and hang it upside down in the basement or a dark closet. Don't put green tomatoes in the refrigerator, and don't put

them on the windowsill. They don't like cold, and they don't like light when they're ripening this way. Wrapping them in newspaper and storing them is acceptable, but they often come out tasting more like newspaper than like vine-ripened tomatoes.

Disease and insects often assail tomatoes. The best defence against both is good soil and careful watering. Hornworms, if they appear, are easy to spot and pick off by hand because they're large and usually not very numerous. They're also spectacularly ugly, and I take a certain perverse pleasure in splattering them on the sidewalk. Leafhoppers and aphids can be controlled with tomato dust or insecticidal soap spray. Blossom-end rot, or tomato blight, is a horrible disease and shouldn't show up if your soil is not too acidic and your watering is careful. If it does appear, remove the diseased plant altogether.

A strategically designed vegetable patch incorporates raised beds and staked plants like the raspberry bushes at the rear and allows for successive plantings of such crops as lettuce. The wooden structures form the edges of the beds and also act as supports for plastic or glass coverings for early plantings that need protection from the elements.

Recommending tomato varieties is something I do very tentatively, because local conditions are so important. But generally, 'Roma' seems to be the best of the paste tomatoes, 'Subarctic Plenty' is the best of the tomatoes adapted for extremely short seasons, and 'Early Girl' and 'Ball's Extra Early' are reliable midsized early varieties. I have a special fondness for 'Sweet Million,' a recent improvement on 'Sweet 100.' Both are extraordinarily flavourful and vigorous cherry-type varieties. The Campbell family of tomatoes seems particularly sweet and reliable. 'Big Boy' is an excellent beefsteak variety.

□   *Turnips, Rutabagas and Kohlrabi*

Turnips are white, rutabagas are yellow-orange, and kohlrabi—which are not considered turnips but really are— are green or purple. They all have a similar taste, and each requires similar conditions to thrive. Fairly generous soil temperatures are required for germination, but they tend to bolt in hot weather. Consequently, the best time to plant them is in midsummer. I've found them rather difficult to cultivate, particularly turnips, to which soil maggots and nearly every other garden pest seem to gravitate. Turnip greens are

edible and something of a gourmet treat. Make sure your soil is well limed, because turnips like a high pH, and add a generous sprinkling of 5 percent granular diazinon when you plant.

Some people suggest using diatomaceous earth to protect turnips and other insect-susceptible root crops. Diatomaceous earth is a white powder made from the fossilized exoskeletons of tiny diatoms and is used in the manufacture of specialty paints. As long as it never rains and you never water your garden, it might do the trick. Even then, however, I suspect that it just makes for bugs with scars on their tummies. I know that scars are supposed to make your body more interesting, but I'm pretty sure that earthworms don't feel this way. Other gardeners may disagree, but I wonder whether diatomaceous earth isn't more effective in killing earthworms than garden pests.

I've had decent success growing kohlrabi, which, despite its weird appearance, can be extraordinarily delicious fresh from the garden. It is prone to clubroot, so watch out. Rutabagas are so cheap in the supermarket that it's almost pointless to go through the agony of fending off all their enemies to grow them yourself.

BERRIES IN A SMALL GARDEN

□

In a compact garden, fruit trees are planted as much for shade and aesthetic effect as for the fruit they produce, so I will reserve my discussion of them for the section on trees (see pages 86-88). Berries—raspberries, strawberries, blueberries, currants and gooseberries—are very much a part of the vegetable garden. Because the plants are rarely attractive and often present special problems in a small garden, however, my cynical advice is to forget about growing berries. (That's also my advice about potatoes, though, and it normally falls on deaf ears.) Since berry lovers are usually a determined bunch and willing to take risks in order to give

their favourites a try, I will outline the difficulties each of them presents.

□   *Blueberries*

Blueberries are acid-loving bog plants that don't enjoy the company of other plants. Unless you're prepared to turn your back garden into a genuine bog, don't even try to grow blueberries. I say this as a passionate blueberry lover who has killed half a dozen expensive blueberry plants trying to ignore my own advice.

□   *Currants and Gooseberries*

A little prettier than raspberries, currant and gooseberry shrubs are still not going to win any beauty contests. Unless you're crazy about them (and some people are) and willing to pay a fair amount of attention to their upkeep, they aren't a good choice for planting in a compact garden.

◻ *Raspberries and Blackberries*

Raspberry canes aren't pretty, and in a small garden, there are rarely any unused sunny corners in which to hide them, as is the practice in Rolling Acres. If you have such a place, by all means, fill it with raspberries. They're less troubled by diseases or bugs (if not human marauders) than are ground-hugging strawberries, and you can get a decent yield out of a relatively small space. Check around to find the best variety for your local conditions.

Raspberries do better when contained, which you can do effectively with five-foot 2-by-2 stakes and baling wire. In the spring, clean out about half the older canes to let the new ones up and out. Good luck.

Blackberries are near relatives of raspberries, but you have to be more careful with them, because there are two kinds. The domesticated strain is a little less vigorous and hardy than raspberries are, and the yields will be smaller. The wild strain, which is an accidental European import that has become a small-scale ecological disaster in some regions, can often be found in vacant lots and along road margins where the climate is relatively mild. Once established, they are nearly impossible to get rid of, and because the bushes are armed with thorns as nasty as those of the most bloodthirsty rosebush, you may bleed to death before you can wipe them out. Stick with raspberries.

◻ *Strawberries*

I've tried to grow strawberries in a number of locations and have never had much success. Strawberries are assailed by nearly every garden pest imaginable, starting with leafhoppers and running right through to small children, medium-sized children and adults. Nearly every creature that inhabits or visits the garden thinks that strawberries are delicious, and therein lies the chief problem: everything and everyone wants to eat your strawberries just as much as you do.

That isn't the only problem. Strawberries thrive best in acid-rich soils that must be extremely well drained. If that requirement isn't met, a quite startlingly wide assortment of diseases can emerge, the most common and debilitating of which is crown rot. Different strains of strawberries produce differently in different climatic conditions, so find out from your local garden centre (or from a neighbour with a foolishness similar to your own) which are the most productive varieties in your area. Stay away from the ever-bearing strains. In a small garden, ever-bearing usually means you'll be able to harvest one strawberry a month.

Unless you want to devote a substantial part of your garden to them, don't expect much yield. On the other hand, if you don't devote a large area, you'll find that small-garden pests will get most of them, particularly if you don't spray. Then again, if you put in a big patch, they will attract thieves and friendly marauders. Be sure to pick off the trailing suckers (they're the means by which strawberries most easily propagate), or you'll get even fewer berries. See what I'm saying? You can't win.

I hope I've talked you out of growing strawberries, but if I haven't, here are two suggestions for the stubborn: One is to grow them vertically, using a large oak barrel with a number of three-inch holes drilled into the top three-quarters of its surface. Fill the barrel with a peat-, vermiculite- and manure-enriched soil mixture, and plant individual strawberry plants in the holes together with a batting of sphagnum moss. Set the barrel atop some bricks, and drill drainage holes in the bottom. You will have to be very careful to maintain moisture

◻ ◻ ◻ ◻ ◻

GUERRILLA GARDENING

Gardening as a form of urban renewal or civic renovation doesn't necessarily have to be done on a community basis, and it needn't even be done in an organized fashion. If you're not the sort of person who likes to wait around for someone else to organize your life, try your hand at guerrilla gardening. I've been doing it for years, without ever being arrested or charged with trespassing. With just a few seeds and a hand trowel, you can sometimes get spectacular results. I've been decorating baseball backstops and industrial chain-link fences with my leftover sweet pea, scarlet runner and other pole bean seeds for about 15 years. The seeds don't always do well (I'd estimate my success rate at about 20 percent), but when they do, there's an immense satisfaction to be had. You'll be making the world a slightly better place, and just think of what our cities would be like if one person in a hundred did this every spring.

levels in the barrel. It will be a daily task. The second tip is to plant alpine strawberries in a sunny, well-drained rock garden or in the herb garden. The yield will be minuscule, but alpine strawberries possess a unique flavour that no domestic strain can even begin to come close to.

RESPONSIBLE COMMUNITY GARDENING

An increasingly popular option for city dwellers who want to grow vegetables or just get their hands into some reasonably organic muck is to join a community gardening association. Depending on which part of the continent you live in and the strength and progressiveness of your municipal government, you will find community gardens in a startling variety of environments and organized in equally diverse ways.

In American cities that suffer from serious urban decay, community gardening has become a form of green radical political action. In Chicago's Maxwell Street slum area, an organization called the MaxWorks Co-op has been taking over derelict properties and "greening" them with small gardens and other ad hoc plantings that have literally transformed the slum. Enlightened city governments in many other cities are specifically assigning derelict and otherwise unused plots of land for semipermanent use as community gardens, frequently with spectacular horticultural and social benefits.

The individual plots available generally aren't all that large (they are rarely bigger than 10 by 10 feet), but their biggest attraction is that they cost next to nothing, and the basic requirements — such as water, compost and manure — are cheaply and easily acquired because they are shared by a group. You can grow whatever you want in your plot, within reason, and vandalism is rare because the gardens are under grassroots control. If you want to grow vegetables but find that your private space is too small or that conditions make it too difficult, community gardens are an option worth looking into. An added bonus is that you'll meet some awfully nice people, often with similar interests and different knowledge.

AN ESSENTIAL HERB GARDEN

I'm a great believer in herb gardens in small spaces, because herbs offer a mix of the best qualities of vegetables, perennials and annual flowers. Herbs are usually attractive, compact plants. Most of them blossom profusely, even if the flowers aren't terribly showy, and they're almost always extremely aromatic. Since store-bought fresh ones are very expensive, herbs are also a good dollar-saving crop, and a sheaf of mixed herbs makes a fine summer gift and an acceptable prop for your trips up and down the alley. And if you're a serious cook, a herb garden is an absolute must.

SETTING UP

Herbs, particularly the perennial varieties, require a sunny location. If you have enough room for a separate bed, dig it deep, make sure the soil is adequately sweetened with lime and has been given an extra dose of humus, and raise the beds if you can.

Location in the garden is an important consideration as well. Once established, the successful herb bed should get a lot of traffic, so try to position it only a step away from the kitchen. If that isn't possible, place a few of your favourite herbs in pots outside the door.

Don't make your herb bed so wide that you can't easily reach every plant in it. A fine clump of Greek oregano or marjoram won't be of much use if you have to trample several other herbs to get at it. If your climate is warm enough that a majority of your herbs can winter over, plant the bed entirely with perennials, removing plants as they get woody and replacing them with younger, more vigorous specimens.

□ *THE BEST HERBS TO GROW*

What you plant in your herb garden should depend on three factors: which herbs will grow well in your climate, which ones you use most in the kitchen and which ones give you—and your guests—the greatest olfactory and visual pleasure. Garlic and chives, for instance, do well in the herb garden, particularly members of the chive family, all of which produce very pretty blossoms if they're left uncut. (For a fuller discussion of garlic and chives, see pages 57 and 60.) The following is a list of some of my favourites.

□ *Basil*

Basil is such a terrific annual herb that it deserves special mention, as well as special treatment. I grow this sun-loving aromatic outside the herb garden because I grow so much of it. It's supposed to be very tender and difficult, but I haven't found that to be the case. It does take some special techniques, but no more so than tomatoes.

Basil as a bedding plant is quite expensive, so if you can, start your own indoors from seed around mid-March. I use sectioned peat pots in plastic seed trays, putting the trays on top of the fridge until the seeds germinate and then moving them to a cooler location under growing lights until they're ready for the garden. In late April or early May, I build a tent frame for them in the garden (mine is about three by four feet and about three feet high at the crown) and cover it with six-mil plastic. About a week later, when the soil inside the tent has warmed thoroughly and dried somewhat, I set the seedlings out on four-inch centres inside the tent. I know that's about three weeks earlier than you're supposed to plant basil, but the tent protects the seedlings from the elements more than adequately. I leave

the tent up until mid- or late June, by which time I can begin to harvest the basil. By carefully pinching off the tops of the plants before they begin to flower, I keep my basil going all summer and into September. Once established, it requires little care beyond occasional watering and fertilizing with a high-nitrogen fertilizer.

You'd never believe the amount of basil I harvest weekly during the hottest part of the summer, so I won't even bother to boast. I use a lot of my crop fresh in pesto sauce, which I then freeze for winter use, but I also dry basil, freeze it, use it for garnishes in salads and give a lot of it away. One summer a few years ago, I actually sold several garbage bagfuls of it to one of the local pasta shops for $2 a pound. I'm not sure if it can be calculated with absolute accuracy, but I suspect that I get greater production out of my basil patch than from any other spot in my garden.

□ *Cilantro (Coriander)*

Because the cilantro you buy in shops is actually Chinese coriander and does not readily form seeds, I prefer to grow domestic coriander in rows so that I can harvest the greens and also obtain a sizable seed crop at the end of the season. A four-foot row of coriander will provide a quart jar of seed. That may seem excessive for a single household, but I use a lot of it. Coriander is a basic ingredient in homemade curries, where I am generous with it. I also use it as a supplement or alternative to pepper.

I have another handy tip: If you fill your pepper grinder with a 50-50 mix of coriander and black pepper, no one will be able to tell the difference. (You will also be helping our balance of trade, and you'll be saving the world from those disastrous pepper-tanker spills they're not telling us about.)

Maturing coriander plants need a little support. Prop them up with two stakes and a piece of string. Harvest as the first seeds begin to turn yellow, and hang the plants upside down indoors,

preferably in the kitchen, where their aroma will fill the air. If you like to have a steady supply of coriander leaves, which are a standard garnish in many Asian and Latin American dishes, seed the garden throughout the summer as spots become available. Coriander doesn't seem to care much about full sun, so you can plant it in less-than-prime locations.

☐   *Lemon Balm*

Lemon balm looks a little like sage and is probably a relative, but it is even more fun to twist between your fingers to release the lemon scent. Some people make a tonic out of it, as they do with lemon verbena.

The silver of the artemisia and sage doesn't quite offset the damage done by the yellow flowers planted in this front-yard herb garden, but it is nevertheless a welcoming, sunny spot. The brick walkway allows the gardener access for cutting and tending the beds.

☐   *Mint*

For many people, mint is an essential garden herb. It comes in a considerable range of types, and it has an even wider range of culinary uses. I use fresh peppermint as a garnish, and I wouldn't cook peas picked fresh from the garden without adding a sprig of mint. Its most common use, however, is in tea.

Peppermint is the most common and vigorous mint, and in most locales, it is a perennial. The flavour of spearmint is a little more subtle, and the plant it-

self is nearly as hardy as peppermint. There are about a dozen exotic and less hardy mints, each of which looks and tastes a little different.

As far as I can see, the only thing wrong with mint is that it spreads. In a small space, that can be the kiss of death. If you have a tiny herb bed, you'll have to plant your mint in a container to keep the roots from escaping. If they do get out, they'll spread through the bed with an enthusiasm rivalling that of wild morning glory, and they're nearly as difficult to eradicate.

Putting mint in pots can cause its own set of problems, however. If you don't pay attention to them, the plants will dry out during hot spells or drown when it rains. I get around this by burying my mints in five-gallon black plastic pots, one-third filled with gravel. I set them into the ground with the rims slightly above the level of the surrounding soil. Each spring, I lift out the big pots and check the roots. If they've made their way out of the pot, I remove the plant, perform extensive root surgery and set both plant and pot back as they were. The spreading problem is most likely with peppermint and spearmint, but if your winters are mild, you should employ the technique with

all mints. With the more exotic strains, you can use a smaller (two-gallon) pot.

☐ *Oregano and Marjoram*

Oregano and marjoram are close relatives and act much the same in both the garden and the kitchen. They're very vigorous and tend to require more control than nurturing. If you let them go to seed, they will self-sow and turn into weeds—again, a dangerous thing in a compact garden.

Both oregano and marjoram are best harvested at the early stages of blooming. Cut them back to the roots between 11 o'clock in the morning and 1 o'clock in the afternoon, when their oils are most active. Then tie the cut plants together, and hang them in sheaves in a cool, dark spot to dry. In Vancouver, homegrown oregano is not as strong as the commercial stuff, perhaps because as a native of the Mediterranean, it

needs a lot of summer heat to acquire full flavour. I get around this by doubling the quantities called for in recipes.

☐ *Parsley*

I can't live without fresh parsley during the summer. Although it is technically a biennial, I treat it as if it were an annual, spotting homegrown parsley seedlings throughout the garden whenever a space becomes available.

☐ *Rosemary*

Where I live, quite a few tender perennial herbs will winter over. My personal favourite is rosemary, which, if carefully sheltered from cold winter winds, cheerfully grows into a decent-sized shrub. It is highly aromatic, has gorgeous pink blossoms in late spring and has several hundred culinary uses. It can be harvested at any time. Rosemary is easily propagated from stem

A simple way of creating a garden with several different elevations is to group potted plants within the bed itself. In this arrangement, Bibb lettuce and basil in containers are interplanted with trailing nasturtiums and nicotiana.

cuttings (on new wood), so each year, I root a dozen or so cuttings to give away to friends and neighbours and to replenish any losses among my own plants. To protect some of my rosemary from heavy winter frosts, I always pot one specimen in sterilized soil at the end of the summer and bring it in for the winter, where it makes a prettier display than most potted plants. If I lived in a colder climate, I'd keep a big one in a 14-inch pot, bury it in the garden each spring and bring it indoors in the fall.

I can't resist divulging one of my cooking secrets so that you will understand why I insist on growing rosemary in such large quantities. When barbecuing, I drop a couple of large sprigs atop the coals and close the lid. What emerges will astound a professional chef. It is particularly good with lamb and fish. Fresh halibut steaks cooked this way are so delicious that they can send even those who dislike fish into gastronomic fibrillations.

□   *Sage*

Like thyme, sage comes in a wide range of shapes and colours. It is a must for saltimbocca, which is arguably the most delicious of the many things Italian chefs can do with veal. Stay with the standard Dalmatian sage, which is hardier and has a superior flavour. It can be dried in the same way as other herbs, but it is better than the ground commercial sage only when it is fresh. If you leave a sage plant in the garden uncut for a year, it will flower, and its blossoms are quite interesting.

□   *Thyme*

Thyme is another of my favourites. I generally start a couple of six-compartment containers of it from seed under my growing lights each spring and use the seedlings to replace the older plants in the garden. This gives me a chance to cultivate and replenish the soil.

There seem to be about a million or so different varieties of thyme, all of them aromatically distinct and visually different. The only ones I can't distinguish between are unfortunately the two that count the most—English thyme and French thyme, which are the most useful culinary types. Both seem equally hardy and flavourful. (I'm told that French thyme has narrower leaves, but that hasn't done me any good in helping to tell them apart.)

I always have a couple of lemon thyme plants in my herb bed because I love the smell of this herb and the way it makes whitefish taste. A little more delicate than English or French, lemon thyme does not propagate easily from cuttings, and seeds are impossible to obtain. Lemon thyme can be acquired as a bedding plant from better garden centres. (I have friends in Ontario, though, who claim that once established, this plant has made legitimate attempts to overthrow the order of the garden. I can't say whether that's a regional difference or not.)

Plant other thyme species mainly for decorative purposes. You can judge how hardy they are with absolute accuracy by the closeness of their resemblance to English or French thyme. The other varieties are not culinary herbs, and I think they're more appropriate in the rock garden than in the herb bed. I've noticed that the woolly varieties (there are quite a few) are favourite hiding spots for slugs, who seem to like snacking on them before they head off for bigger game. Since none of my relatives are snail-family members, I'm not convinced that I've been missing a major gourmet treat. I eventually moved such plants from the herb bed to the rock garden, where the slugs didn't waste any time finishing them off.

All thymes, except French and English, should be harvested and dried in the same way as oregano. Harvesting and pruning should be done around noon hour in spring while they're in bloom. You can also harvest small sprigs for cooking anytime during the season without harming the plants.

THE MIXED GARDEN

Early spring flowers emerge from

a green ground cover of periwinkle

and violets in the grassless yard, left.

Right: sweet-scented alyssum is planted

beneath the somewhat more attention-

grabbing tuberous begonias.

Human beings do not live by bread alone, and kohlrabi, tomatoes and basil won't fulfill all our needs either. A few of my richer acquaintances seem to live for BMWs and artichokes, but I don't envy them. BMWs and artichokes have to be imported, and it's about time we all stopped importing our lives and looked around to see how interesting our own environments are and how much we can—and perhaps must—start doing to improve them.

I'm not winding up for another sermon on ecology—really. Although my chapter on vegetable gardening may have given the impression that I've turned my backyard into a food factory, that impression isn't correct. I did attempt that with some of my earlier gardens, but in the past decade or so, I've come around to a more moderate view of many things, and my approach to gardening has evolved accordingly.

Cities are extraordinarily complex environments, and the more densely populated the neighbourhood you live in, the more complexity there will be. This complexity ought to be embraced. It is a living rebuttal to the monocultural intentions which our corporate

systems seem to want to impose on us, and I've come to believe that gardens can be a powerful component of a good neighbourhood, reflecting that complexity. In other words, we ought to be doing mixed gardening.

By mixed gardening, I mean gardening for aesthetic effect as well as for food production. Achieving aesthetic coherence in a small garden requires some skill, because the object of the exercise is exactly the same as it is in much larger gardens: to create a satisfying display of colour, texture and landscaping by combining blossoms and foliage, both of which change with the seasons. Given generous amounts of money and space, one can accomplish this with relative ease because the tableau one is working with is much more forgiving. In a small urban garden, however, it is going to be difficult because you usually see the entire garden at once.

It isn't impossible, though. The basic rules are similar. It is just that your options are more restricted. I'll begin by going over the basic rules and how to apply them. Then I'll discuss ways of putting them into proper perspective and ways of bending them. But first, indulge me a little.

Until a few years ago, I thought real gardeners only grew vegetables. I was, I suppose, unconsciously giving in to a bit of Oedipal game playing, siding with my mother against my father. When I was a child, my parents split the gardening duties right down the middle. My mother grew all the vegetables, and my father just seemed to putter around. I never thought much about why they did this. I guess it was part of the usual division of labour between husbands and wives in those days. Men worked in the outside world, and when they came home, they got to play. Around

A curved pathway is laid through an ornamental and edible patio garden that is bordered by latticed fencing and climbing shrubs. In the shadier portion of the garden is a wide sweep of impatiens.

STREET-SMART

If you live in a crowded neighbour-hood, one of the things you don't want to do is make your garden border look too conspicuous, at least not at the front. You are part of a streetscape that is, and should be, regarded as common ground. In my neighbour-hood, several of the adjacent proper-ties have boxwood hedges along the street front. I've planted boxwood along the front sidewalk too—as a courtesy to my neighbours and to con-tribute to the streetscape's aesthetic coherence. If the common thing had been white picket fences, I'd have gone along with that as well, even though I rather dislike white picket fences. (There's another, less altruis-tic reason for staying with the street-scape standard: conspicuous houses are often the ones that are most likely to be robbed and vandalized.)

What I do inside my boxwood hedge is, of course, entirely of my choosing. And back gardens are different. They should be as varied as the individuals who create them—provided that one's individualism doesn't restrict a neigh-bour's gardening options.

the home, women were in charge—or at least they did most of the work.

I thought my father's gardening prac-tices and interests were silly. They were clearly less successful and productive than my mother's. Of course, he didn't spend nearly as much time at it, and when he did, he planted trees, shrubs and flowers—stuff that seemed to have no real purpose. A few of his choices thrived in that cold climate, but a great many more did not. As disaster after di-saster overtook his gardening endeav-ours, my affinity for my mother's veg-etable garden became a prejudice. My father had a little success with crab apple trees and with some of his shrubs, but this intensely businesslike and pragmatic man's attempts to grow flow-ers struck me as slightly peculiar and very much out of character.

It isn't that I didn't like flowers. As a child, I was partial to pansies and peo-nies, and as I grew older, I developed very strong floral likes and dislikes. A woman I lived with collected blue crys-tal vases as a hobby (we parted com-pany because I had decided she wanted to make it her career), and for several summers, we cruised the alleys in our neighbourhood for blossoms to fill the vases. When we parted, she generously left behind part of the blue crystal col-lection, along with a book of surpris-ingly precise instructions on what kinds and colours of blossoms go with the vases. To this day, I have a love of blue and purple flowers and an aversion to yellow and orange ones. But until a few years ago, it had never occurred to me to grow my own.

My current neighbours finally kin-dled my interest in growing flowers. Al-most all of them have mixed gardens, and it soon became apparent to me that I couldn't go around forever being the, er, midnight pruner. I'd developed a taste for cut flowers, and it began to dawn on me that I'd have to grow my own if I didn't want to end up on the business end of someone's pitchfork— or in jail. It was fine in the early spring,

when the flowering trees and shrubs need a little pruning, but the truth is that I'm not quite the risk-taking night owl I once was, and anyway, playing Oedipus Gardener can't go on indefi-nitely—even gardeners have to grow up.

As I looked around my neighbour-hood, I began to notice how differently each of my neighbours approached the cultivation of blossoms and foliage. One of my Portuguese neighbours pre-fers roses, and there are few other blos-soming plants in his yard. Archie and Phyllis, the neighbourhood's neatest and most dedicated mixed gardeners, prefer boxwood hedging and creeping plants that require a minimum of up-keep in their shady front garden. But in the backyard flowerbeds, they com-bine delphiniums, peonies and fox-gloves with a riotous selection of low-growing petunias, trailing lobelia and geraniums, which they grow almost ex-clusively in large pots and other con-tainers. My Chinese neighbours, on the other hand, grow only three flow-ers: dahlias, chrysanthemums and a strain of deep purple cosmos for which they have been saving their own seeds. Each year, their cosmos plants are a little smaller, but the blossoms are a lit-tle deeper in colour and the plants seem to hold their blossoms later into the season. Until the cosmos begin to bloom in midsummer, their yard is without flowers except for the unruly border of tall flowering shrubs that separates our two yards at the front. But as fall approaches, the yard be-comes a brilliant show of colour.

None of the floral displays in my neighbourhood is likely to find its way into *House & Garden* magazine, but there are weeks at a time when the en-tire neighbourhood might make it—if one half-closes one's eyes and ignores the fact that no plan is in place.

No two gardeners are the same, just as no two gardens are the same. You may want a garden that combines in-teresting foliage and flower arrange-ments with a reasonable production of vegetables, as I do. You may want to concentrate on floral displays as Archie and Phyllis do. Or you may want a heavily landscaped privacy garden that creates the illusion of completeness and isolation. Provided you're not the sort of person who wants a garden with no upkeep and that you want more from your backyard than a secure spot to park a gravel truck, you're still reading the right book. Throughout this section, I'll assume that your ideal garden mix is somewhere between mine, which is oriented toward vegetable gardening, and Archie and Phyllis's, which leans heavily toward floral display. In other words, you're interested in growing some pretty plants, and you're not afraid of having people see them.

□ *PRIVACY AND COMPACT GARDENS*

For several good reasons, gardening for complete privacy is not my preference. First, achieving visual privacy in a small urban garden is probably a hopeless cause. I'm against bunkers, which are your best bet if you're really set on having a private garden. Besides, someone can always see what you're doing anyway. Outdoor spaces in crowded localities ought to be integrated into the neighbourhood's overall sitescape as well as into its social fabric. That requires a deliberate openness and tolerance – a willingness to see and be seen – to be, in a deeper sense, conversant.

I know this contradicts the central goal of middle-class life: to acquire enough property and technology that you don't have to see or talk to anyone. But since the whole consumerist middle-class enterprise isn't working anyway (and is likely to result in the destruction of the planet if it isn't stopped), I've given it up in my garden, and I'm willing to prescribe the same for you.

□ *CHOOSING YOUR OWN AESTHETIC*

Gardener or not, nearly everyone has favourite flowers and colours. These highly individual preferences should form the backbone of your decorative garden. Remember that you are gardening for your own delight, that you have limited time and that you're not trying to win awards or one-up your neighbours. So treat yourself, and forget about the idea of a perfect garden. Create an interesting one instead, and don't expect anyone else to find it as interesting as you do.

I had this drummed into me a couple of years back. As I said, I've developed a weakness for blue flowers, and I'd filled my shady front yard with what I thought was a striking and rather cunning array of blues and near blues: deep blue lobelia along the borders of the beds; potted petunias on the porch steps and walkways; pansies, Siberian bellflowers and grape hyacinths elsewhere. I was out digging with my hand cultivator one morning when a neighbour stopped by the gate. He scratched his chin ruminatively, and I smiled back, ready to accept the flood of compliments I believed were richly deserved. "Do you know," he said, as if he were pointing out an error I had inexplicably fallen into without realizing it, "that you haven't got a damned thing here but blue flowers?"

□ *DESIGNING A MIXED GARDEN*

In a vegetable garden, design ought to serve production. But with a mixed garden, you'll need to juggle a number of goals, and the design parameters will be more complex and more elastic. You'll want your design to express your horticultural likes and dislikes, of course, but you'll also want to plan for more than a single activity. You may want a spot for quiet rest and contemplation, you'll want a work area for potting plants, you might enjoy a spot specifically for aromatics or an eye-level visual display, and you may need an area where you can safely wrestle with pet alligators and children. Other more purely aesthetic considerations involve

Working with what you have means more than simply taking advantage of available light: this gardener uses the steps into the backyard to show off a variety of potted plants. The nearby wall absorbs heat and creates a friendly environment for sun-loving plants below and cascading vines planted above.

things like balance of line, colour, texture, plant size and light characteristics. As you gaze around your garden, your eyes should be able to stroll and rest, not bounce, lurch and come to an abrupt halt. You don't have to stick to the design you settle on, but having one will help you begin to satisfy formal and aesthetic longings. Eventually, you'll settle on your own combination of the following possibilities:

☐ continuous floral display

☐ displaying a particular blossom, family of blossoms or combinations of various blossoms

☐ displaying a single colour or combination of colours

☐ fragrance

☐ minimum upkeep

The most general concept of mixed gardening is fairly straightforward. There are basically two kinds of flowers: annuals and perennials. Annuals generally bloom for one growing season and stop flowering once they set seed. If you want to keep them blooming throughout the summer, you must pinch off the spent blossoms, a technique called dead-heading that encourages the plants to flower again. The role of annuals in a small garden is to provide colour from spring through fall. (There are also biennials, plants that establish themselves in the garden as green plants the first year, then flower and set seed the following growing season. For ease of gardening, it's a good idea to consider these as annuals, buying them in their second year of growth and transplanting them as you would annuals—weeding and bed maintenance tend to dislocate seedlings that might emerge from dropped seeds.)

Perennials survive from year to year, sometimes happy to be left alone and sometimes profiting from division and

79

relocation. Each has a flowering period of about three weeks every year, sometime between early spring and fall, depending on the plant, and usually cannot be persuaded to flower at any other time. Other permanent members of your garden that will contribute to floral display are spring and summer bulbs and flowering trees and shrubs, most of which bloom sometime between early spring and midsummer.

I could burden you with a thousand other design considerations, but quite frankly, I've never really understood how to apply them reliably, and I'm more or less convinced that applying them abstractly is unnecessary. For a beginner, a lot of complex design factors can be very intimidating, and I've seen more than one person give up in the face of the implied demands. I've tried throughout this book to stick to the specific: tips I can verify from my own experience. I could point out, for instance, that colour is affected by available light (cloudy days intensify the colours of blossoms, while the midday sun tends to flatten hues). But I'm more likely to recommend that you grow 'Crystal Palace' lobelia and that you have a look at them around twilight, when the blue becomes almost magically brilliant. For the most part, the theoretical principles of garden design, it seems to me, are things we eventually absorb with experience. If some of us never quite master them, there's nothing wrong in that.

☐   *FINDING OUT WHAT YOU CAN GROW*

Beware of those elegant coffee-table books that show you how inadequate your taste is or how economically poor and horticulturally unskilled you really are. The best ones are a valuable source

Ceramic tiles provide an appealing and smooth flooring for a private backyard sitting area bordered by planted herbs, tomatoes and petunias. A reminder: when laying what you hope will be permanent tiles, be sure you make drainage part of the plan. Otherwise, that lazy morning coffee on the patio after a summer rain may involve rubber boots.

PLANNING BEHIND

If you've just bought a house and, like most new homeowners, are in the process of sorting out necessary renovations, make sure you account for your garden in your plans. My friend with the long, skinny two-storey house and descending backyard came within a hair of building a large deck that would have effectively blocked entry to the backyard for anything larger than a small child with a plastic bucket. A prescient friend (obviously not me) helped her revise the deck plan to allow adequate access to the back garden. This improved her renovation plan in several ways, made her a happier person and allowed for the fairly extensive soil enrichment the garden needed. It also eliminated the bucket-brigade party that would otherwise have been necessary to get new soil into the garden. You don't need freeway-style access, of course, but do make sure your renovation plans acknowledge both the presence of the garden and a way to get things into and out of it.

of good ideas, but they can make you very depressed. I've learned to read these books without envy, because I know that the people who produced the gardens in them are either much harder-working than I'm prepared to be or they're crazy—or both. Think of these gardens the way you used to think of fairy tales when you were a kid, and you'll be able to enjoy them more. They're like fairy tales, and their reality is, well, partial. Fairy tales don't talk about how hard the peasants had to work or about all the days when the castle was damp and shabby.

Most major cities have botanical gardens, and these are a valuable resource in deciding what to grow. You should remember, however, that like the castles in fairy tales, these establishments have full-time gardening staffs and hefty budgets. To start off and protect tender species, they also have large greenhouses that cost more than your home to build and maintain.

□ MY FAVOURITE FAIRY-TALE GARDEN

Three years ago, at one of our Sunday-afternoon baseball games, Jim, one of the guys on my team, asked me if I'd come over to his house after the game. He and his significant other, Baerbel, who'd recently emigrated from her native Germany, had just moved into a small place not far from mine, and they both wanted to do some gardening. I said, "Sure," and popped a few questions about what kind of space he had and what he knew about gardens. He admitted to having a life-long case of black thumb that was so advanced he could kill a houseplant simply by looking at it. He also noted that his small gardening space wasn't exactly ideal. "It has about a foot of sawdust covering it," he said, "and it's full of some sort of vine that has lots of underground roots."

He wasn't exaggerating. Except for its southern orientation, everything about his 15-by-30-foot garden space was a beginner's nightmare. The sawdust cover

was close to 18 inches deep, and the vine was wild morning glory, also known as bindweed. The previous tenant had kept a large and vicious dog in the yard, and apparently the only thing in the neighbourhood that wasn't afraid of the dog was the morning glory. We dug a few holes to see what was underneath the sawdust and how thoroughly and deeply the morning glory had penetrated the soil beneath. "You're going to have to remove all this," I said, pointing to the sawdust, "and you'll have to get all the morning glory roots, or they'll take over whatever you plant."

Jim didn't flinch. "Okay," he said. "What else?"

Since the soil beneath the sawdust didn't look great, I suggested that he bring in a load of mushroom manure, lime it, fertilize it and dig it in. "That'll get you to the point where you can begin to garden." Again, he didn't flinch.

Over the next few months, I had several conversations with Jim about any number of gardening subjects. He wanted to know how to set up an indoor system of growing lights, and he had endless questions about the hardiness and light requirements of different flowers. I answered as best I could and kept my suggestions to a minimum. (Jim has always been strong-minded, and I knew he'd make up his mind about what to do in his own way.)

Over the next two years, our conversations changed. The question-and-answer sessions became give-and-take technical discussions. Jim's version of my growing-light system is bigger than mine, and his interest in (and knowledge of) plant genetics quickly outdistanced my own, particularly on the subject of annual flowers. He's been experimenting with a strain of domesticated morning glory (this past spring, he produced 300 seedlings from seeds he'd collected), and he's had considerable success with petunias and a number of other temperamental species. He and Baerbel are equal gardening partners, and they're a source of information to anyone who asks. They are also the objects of considerable admiration.

Their garden is now a wonder. It isn't a *House Beautiful* wonder, because the house they live in is rented, and Jim isn't the sort who will spend a lot of money building elegant fencing on a property that someone can sell out from under them. But they've transformed the entire place, and the centrepiece is the 15-by-30-foot former dog run. It has a small rock garden bursting with a range of exotic trailing ground covers and succulents, and the rest of the garden is an apparently chaotic symphony of annuals and perennials —as well as a couple of tomato and cucumber plants.

Their most astonishing achievement, though, is the array of morning glories. In the summer, they cover the entire north side of the garden and large sections of the adjoining carport, stretching from the garden to the railing of the balcony that overlooks the garden. Morning glories are planted in the garden and in a variety of pots, most of them the cheap one-gallon black plastic variety. Jim claims that the morning glories in the pots are earlier and that they produce a wider variety of colours than the soil-planted ones, but he isn't sure why. From the original pinks and mauves, he's produced white, deep purple jet and an assortment of striated blossoms. The last time I was over, he was collecting seeds from favourite colours he'd tagged six weeks ago. "We'll see what happens in the spring," he said. I can hardly wait for the next chapter of this fairy-tale garden.

□   *A NOTE TO BEGINNERS*

Most flowering plants have their origins in tropical and subtropical climates. They've been adapted to our more northerly climates, but most remain fragile, sometimes in unexpected ways. While vegetable gardening often takes little more than some common sense and a willingness to dig, decorative gardening is more difficult. The failures are often more spectacular and discouraging, and you need a certain savvy and organizational ability to get really good at it.

TAPPING A RESOURCE

The climatic-zone map on page 121 will give you a very rough idea of what will grow in your climate. Many gardening encyclopaedias contain marvellously detailed versions of the same thing, with gradient colours and proscriptive warnings about all the horrible disasters that will befall if you ignore them. My view of climatic maps is somewhat different: they will give you a sense of how much trouble it'll be to grow plants that are marginal in your area. That is why the maps are useful. But they certainly aren't the only parameter that governs what you choose to plant.

Your best source of accurate information and ideas is right around you. What your neighbours do is your best indicator of what to grow and how to grow it, particularly if your neighbourhood has been settled for some time. Old gardens aren't just a look into the past. They're a multipaned window onto the future of your own garden. You just need to be interested enough to keep looking and asking.

□   *LIVING HAPPILY WITH YOUR TREES*

Trees are likely to be the most permanent items in your garden, which is something you'll understand perfectly if you've had to begin by removing an old or dead tree from your yard. Trees deserve to be given very careful consideration, because they're going to have a profound effect on everything around them. They're also rather expensive to purchase, and some of the really pretty ones are a lot more expensive than others.

The most basic fact about trees is something that a surprising percentage of otherwise intelligent people forget all about: they grow. Three small trees may seem inconsequential when they are planted. But in 20 years or 10 or even 5, they can dominate a garden, and if they're planted in the wrong place, they can rip up sidewalks, pavements and even house foundations.

Plan your tree plantings very carefully, and base your plans on the demands the trees will make when they are full grown and the effects they will have on their surroundings rather than on their ability to fulfill a short-term need. That way, you can take satisfaction in knowing that you're echoing the strategies employed in the great European gardens, where trees were planted with the understanding that they would not reach their prime for perhaps a century or more. We're the heirs of that kind of foresight. When you plant a tree that you know will look splendid in 20 or 30 years, you're expressing that same faith in the future—and making the right sort of investment in it, even though you may not be the one who ultimately enjoys it.

You, too, can have a garden like this. It won't happen overnight, but long-range planning and early attention to soil quality, bed creation and plant selection will eventually reap big rewards. Lettuce and snapdragons are interplanted with a variety of perennials to the right of this gravel path, while irises, roses, poppies and alyssum grow to the left.

When making a decision about likely specimens to plant, first look around your neighbourhood. You can go a step further by taking the time to wander around your city to see which species of trees you find attractive and in what settings they are growing. Then, having made a plan and a tentative selection of tree species, go to your favourite nursery and price them. I suggest that you also visit the nursery with the largest selection of trees and do a comparative price check. Go directly to the suppliers if they're not too far away. Their trees are likely to be cheaper, but remember, the farther a tree travels unprotected from the elements, the greater the probability of its being damaged in transit. If the tree you're going to plant is reasonably large, have it delivered. Nurseries are experienced at moving trees around and will guarantee a tree's safe delivery and usually its health for a period of time after planting.

If you've decided on a native species for your garden, I don't recommend going out into the woods and digging one up for your yard. Your chances of removing it from its natural environment without seriously damaging its root system are not good, and the government is not fond of individuals doing that sort of thing without paying taxes unless they're giant forestry corporations.

Instead of removing trees from private land, go to your local garden centre and buy your trees. Both you and the trees will have a much better chance of surviving. They will have been moved at least once already, and their roots will be covered with protective materials. (If they aren't, don't make the purchase.)

□ *PLANTING TREES*

One of the chief problems with trees in a small garden is the lateral spreading

To compensate for root trauma when both bare-rooted and balled-and-burlapped trees are transplanted, some people prune back about a third or a quarter of the top growth. But don't simply hack off a third of every branch; prune out damaged, weak or poorly placed branches (the ones that cross others, for instance). Container-grown trees don't need such radical treatment, but it doesn't hurt to do a cleanup when you're transplanting. You should also stake a young tree with a wooden or metal pole. The pole should be at least half the height of the tree and be placed six to eight inches from the trunk on the windward side. Attach the tree to the stake with a heavy cord or a piece of wire that you've threaded through a length of old hose (this keeps the wire or rope from cutting into the bark). Check to see that the wrap isn't choking the tree, and remove it after the tree has established itself—usually in two or three years.

□   *Do's, Don'ts and Other Tips*

□ Do check carefully to make sure the environment in your garden is suitable for the trees or shrubs you want to plant. Some species suffer without very particular site conditions, and a sickly tree can be both an eyesore and a magnet that draws insects and diseases to your garden. With smaller trees and shrubs, be sure the planting location will receive adequate light.

□ Do consult your neighbours if you're thinking of planting a tree that will grow quite large. There's no sure way of negotiating these kinds of arrangements, but it is worth finding out if they have concerns or alternative suggestions. If your plan is sensible and you're not going to re-create the Black Forest at their expense, they probably won't object, and your courtesy may be repaid later on. The fact is that large trees aren't quite personal property: they belong to the neighbourhood.

□ Do look for dwarf varieties of normally large trees and shrubs. They're

of their roots. They rob adjoining soil of nutrients, work their way into sewers and drainage tiles and break up sidewalks and masonry with surprising ease. A tactic that has worked for me has been to encourage a tree's roots to go downward instead of sideways. You can do this by digging an extra-deep planting hole. The general rule of thumb in preparing planting holes for trees and shrubs is to dig a hole three times the size of the rootball. In your small garden, try digging a hole four times the size of the rootball, going straight down for that extra volume. Fill the hole with a mixture of whatever organic materials you have on hand: old sod, compost, well-rotted manure, peat or a combination of these. Remember that if you have a high water table, this won't work very well, because tree roots are not equipped with scuba-diving gear and you yourself may drown while digging the hole. You should also check the rooting propensities of your chosen tree or shrub and its tolerance to water. Some seem to have roots that travel laterally no matter what encouragement you give them to do otherwise. Don't plant such trees in a small garden unless you're willing to live with the consequences.

The tulip-shaped blossoms of the saucer magnolia are a familiar sight in both Canadian and American gardens. City- and shade-tolerant, this tree blooms spectacularly in early spring, temporarily grabbing most of the attention in a small garden.

84

TREE TRIALS

Your choice of trees and the spot in which you've chosen to plant them are final, sort of. You can correct mistakes, but most people never seem to get around to it. Don't ask me why. Probably it has to do with some vestigial genetic circuit from the days when our ancestors lived in trees. In mediaeval Germany, as a matter of fact, tree murder was a capital offence, and the method of execution was far too gory to relate here. Even today, for not so different reasons, cutting down large trees is illegal in several European countries, even on one's own property. Trees are a resource of the entire neighbourhood, and the advantages of having them and the problems they create are inevitably shared.

becoming more common every year and often are more appropriate choices for a compact garden.

□ Don't forget that your neighbours have a moral, if not a legal, right to sunlight. Planting a large or spreading tree beside the vegetable garden next door will eventually get you considerably more than some shade in your yard. It will earn you the permanent antipathy of your neighbour.

□ Don't plant trees or shrubs with large growth habits close to the house. They'll look fine for a few years while they're growing, but eventually, they will crowd or dwarf the building and end up looking terrible themselves.

□ Don't plant trees—such as willow and poplar—or vines with invasive root systems where they have access to your sewers, the drainage tiles of your house or those of your neighbours. You can hire people to clear roots out of your sewer pipes, but it is quite costly and is usually unpleasant as well. Any way you cut it, overflowing toilets and sinks aren't among life's cherished delights. Invasive roots tend to be more of a problem in mild areas, where the sewer pipes are laid relatively shallowly. But even in harsher climates, you'd be amazed at how far down roots will travel to get into a juicy sewer and how easily those roots will penetrate the slightest imperfection in a pipe.

□ Deciduous trees generally afford more summer and less winter shade than evergreens. Judiciously planting a deciduous tree on the south side of your house can help cool the house during the summer and still let in some winter sun. Don't plant evergreens on the south side of your house unless you are willing to lose substantial amounts of sunny garden space to them.

□ Some trees are messier than others. Fruit trees will drop whatever fruit you don't use, which will draw vermin and other refuse eaters such as yellow jackets. Other deciduous trees have less problematic, but still messy, by-products of flower production—seedpods

and catkins, for instance. Some trees leak sap from branches and leaves, which can be especially annoying around sidewalks or driveways where automobiles are parked.

□ Trees that grow very quickly, such as willows, aspens and some of the more vigorous maples, are susceptible to damage from wind and ice.

□ *SOME GOOD TREES FOR SMALL GARDENS*

The trees in the following list have a number of features that make them appropriate for compact gardens across the continent: they are hardy in a wide range of climates, they are tolerant of polluted city conditions, and they generally won't grow taller than 25 to 30 feet. As well, most of them make more than one contribution to your yard—their colour, fruit, form or shade.

□ *Birch*

Healthy and long-lived if planted in well-drained soil, the birch has a number of qualities to recommend it. Its bright green summer foliage and golden autumn leaves give it an instant presence, as will the white bark it develops after five or six years. Its smaller growth habit (it grows to 15 to 20 feet in 5 years and reaches a mature height of 25 to 30 feet in 10 to 15 years) makes it a good choice for the compact garden. It is easily underplanted with ground covers and evergreens (if you're interested in that sort of thing), but you should be cautious about the weeping varieties because their ground-trailing limbs can be magnets for pests.

□ *Flowering Dogwood*

Among the most impressive of all flowering trees, the flowering dogwood bears three-to-five-inch blossoms that last almost a month in midspring. The blossoms are usually white, although there are pink varieties, and the bright red fruit will draw birds to your garden. In fall, the dogwood's leaves turn orange or red, while in winter, the upturned ends of its horizontal branches are swollen with green buds ready for next spring's flowers. It does best in light shade and well-drained, acidic soil.

☐ *Littleleaf Linden*

A great tree for cities, the littleleaf linden is extremely tolerant of air pollution. Its conical shape and relatively dense branches cast welcome shade all summer. A real plus is that its heart-shaped, deep green leaves appear in early spring and stay with the tree until late fall. But a word of caution: it is sometimes attractive to aphids, which, in sucking sap from the leaves, cause a sticky substance to drop from the tree.

☐ *Magnolia*

The saucer, or Chinese, magnolia offers showy six-inch tulip-shaped blossoms of white, pink or purple in early spring. (Star magnolia blooms somewhat later but more profusely with three-inch star-shaped blossoms.) Magnolias are pest-free and tolerant of both shade and the fumes and grime of city air, which makes them good candidates for the urban garden. But a cautionary note: their flowers sometimes open so early that they are nipped by a late frost, so set the tree in an exposed area or on the north side of the house in order to hold back the blossoms' growth until the danger of frost is past.

☐ *Maple*

Most maples are too large for the compact garden, despite the appeal of the shade they provide and their brilliant fall colour. A couple of smaller maple species, however, can be perfect choices for a small space. The Japanese maple (*Acer palmatum*) is a small, graceful, slow-growing tree that has red foliage in spring and fall (some varieties are red in summer as well). The drawbacks are that it is only moderately cold-resistant and it prefers filtered shade.

The paperbark maple (*Acer griseum*) is also a small, slow-growing tree. A native of China, it is best known for its exfoliating bark, which peels back to reveal the fresh growth layer underneath, often showing colours of cinnamon, orange and red.

☐ *Mountain Ash*

The small white flowers that appear on this tree in early summer produce clusters of bright red and orange berries in fall that will attract robins and cedar waxwings to your garden. The mountain ash casts a light, filtered shade that allows underplanting. On the downside, all but the Korean variety are susceptible to borers.

☐ *Russian Olive*

Fast-growing, pest-free and adaptable, the Russian olive has tiny yellow fragrant flowers in early summer. In late summer and early fall, it yields sweet yellow berries that, like those of the mountain ash, are welcomed by birds. Its most distinguishing features are its silver-grey leaves and dark bark. Left unpruned, it will develop as a tall shrub, growing 12 to 15 feet in height. If trained as a tree, it will reach about 25 feet at maturity. Be careful though: despite the illusion of softness created by the foliage of this tree, its bark is covered with two-to-three-inch thorns that are a hazard to the unwary.

☐ *Thornless Honey Locust*

The light, fernlike leaves of this tree make it one of the best bets for any garden. It casts a light, filtered shade under which it is possible to grow a wide variety of plants, and it seems to tolerate any soil conditions as well as city air. A low-maintenance, affordable tree, its leaves actually turn yellow and disintegrate as they blow away in the fall.

☐ *FRUIT TREES*

Fruit-bearing trees are often an excellent choice for a compact garden, particularly if they're chosen wisely. Most of them don't grow ridiculously large (and dwarf varieties are plentiful), all are amenable to pruning and shaping, and nearly all of them bear attractive blossoms in the spring.

Fruit trees do come replete with their own unique set of problems, however. First of all, you'll have to be careful to choose species that are appropriate for your climate. No matter how much you like apricots and peaches, you won't have much luck with an apricot tree on the Canadian Prairies or in the Midwest. Different areas are also subject to growth-stunting viruses, and you may find that certain tree species are actually prohibited in your area.

Fruit trees are the special targets of any number of pests and diseases. To obtain a full and healthy harvest from them, you may have to be willing to spray with a series of oils and toxic and noxious insecticides.

Apples and Pears

Apple trees take a long time to reach bearing maturity, and they're fairly susceptible to diseases and pest attacks. They usually need to be cross-pollinated, but grafting tactics will get you around that (see page 89). I'm a little reluctant to recommend specific apple species. Almost every apple-growing area I've visited has its local favourites, and there are usually good reasons for that. If you live in a very cold climate, try crab apples. They'll grow — and often thrive — where no other apple can survive. They're not much good for eating, but they make superior jellies, are great for rotten crab apple fights and are the most decorative of apple trees.

Pear trees behave in much the same way as apple trees, except that they're slightly less hardy and vigorous. Like apples, they can't be counted on to self-pollinate, so it is better to grow two compatible pear trees.

Cherries

Where climate allows, cherry trees are robust and fast-growing and provide a cloud of white blossoms in the spring. The best sweet cherries — with fruit you can eat straight from the tree — are

probably 'Bing' and 'Van' (deep purple) and 'Queen Anne' (mottled with yellow). 'Montmorency' is the best sour, or pie, cherry. Sour cherry trees are hardier than sweet; they are self-fertile, so you need plant only one; and they grow to about half the size of a sweet cherry, which makes them a good choice for a compact garden.

Birds, particularly starlings, are serious cherry predators. If your tree is small enough, you can cover it with nets; the starlings will land, get caught and strangle themselves — in which case, you'll feel terribly guilty.

Wild cherries, by the way, are much hardier than the domesticated strains, but their fruit is strictly for the birds.

Make sure, when you're selecting a cherry tree, that you don't end up with one of those flowering Japanese cherries. They blossom very prettily, but they don't bear any fruit at all. On the other hand, that may be exactly what you're looking for.

Peaches and Apricots

Peaches need warmer climates than apples, and apricots like it warmer still. Most are self-pollinating, but that's about the only advantage I can think of. If you've got the climate, they produce wonderful fruit, but I don't think the trees are very attractive unless they are in an orchard.

Plums

Plum trees are wonderful candidates for a compact garden because they are smaller than most other fruit trees and because their crops are less likely to be wiped out by insect attacks, diseases and inclement weather. European, or prune, plums are hardier and more vigorous than most of the others, and many types are self-pollinating. My personal favourite is the golden plum, but there are dozens of other varieties worth having a look at. Many of the decorative flowering plums have deep purple leaves and are among the earliest trees to flower in spring.

As always, stick with the local favourites, because there are usually good reasons for the preference. Some species of plum will grow only where crab apples do. A final note: for some reason I've never been able to fathom, small children seem to believe that people who grow plums are witches – so beware.

SHRUBS: MEDIUM AND SMALL

Shrubs are perennials that don't quite make it as trees. They're usually woody and indeterminate and grow no higher than 15 feet. In most cases, proper planting involves the same procedures as with trees. The following is a list of some good flowering shrubs for a compact garden. The species from dogwood to winged spindle tree are all under 6 feet, and the species from forsythia through to sumac grow to between 6 and 15 feet in height.

☐   *Dogwood*

The red-twigged variety (*Cornus alba*) is very hardy, enjoys sun, tolerates shade and has a fondness for moist places. Its colourful bark makes it a real standout in a snow-filled winter yard.

☐   *Potentilla*

A low, hardy shrub with grey-green leaves that prefers full sun and will tolerate almost any soil, potentilla produces white or pale yellow flowers in early summer and sporadically into the fall.

☐   *Rhododendrons and Azaleas*

The variety of rhododendrons and azaleas is almost limitless, but most are only moderately hardy, and you'll have to investigate which are appropriate for

A combination of different-sized trees and shrubs edged with annuals and bulbs is a good bet for a relatively low-maintenance garden. As the plants mature, you can expand the borders and do away with some of the grass most of us hate to cut.

GRAFTING AND PRUNING

Grafting isn't something you want to try yourself. The top of every fruit tree you purchase from a garden centre has already been grafted to its rootstock. Limbs from a compatible species can also be grafted onto your tree, thus ensuring that it will be pollinated. It may be more expensive to buy a tree with this built-in pollinator, but it'll be much cheaper than paying an arborist to come in and graft a suitable branch after you've planted.

In general, use sharp pruning shears (secateurs) to prune relatively new growth, but for anything thicker than three-quarters of an inch, a pruning saw is the answer. The choice of tool will vary depending on how strong your wrists are—I think it's better to use shears than a saw because the cut is cleaner. Make your cut just above a growth node (the place where a bud or branch takes off). Cut on the diagonal (so that moisture does not collect in the cut end) and close to the node (so that there isn't an ugly piece of branch sticking out). And do your pruning at the appropriate time of year for each species (usually in early spring for shrubs which flower on new-season growth and just after flowering for those which bloom on last year's growth). If you're not sure what the appropriate season is, check with an expert.

your locale. They require light shade and very acidic soil. Azaleas come in some thoroughly lurid colours, and companion plantings have been known to die of sheer embarrassment at having to live next to them.

□   *Spiraea*

Distinguished by massive displays of white flowers on gracefully arching stems or flat, bright pink heads on upright stems in late spring, spiraeas do best in full sun but will tolerate light shade and unfriendly soil conditions. Most are hardy and, to round out the package, are generally disease- and pest-resistant.

□   *Weigela*

The arching branches of the weigela are lined with tubular, wide-mouthed, inch-wide flower clusters in white, pink and rosy red. Pest- and disease-resistant in either full sun or partial shade, weigela's weaknesses are that it is only moderately hardy and is a little bit vulgar-looking.

□   *Winged Spindle Tree (Burning Bush)*

The prominent corky ridges on the stems of burning bush make an interesting contribution to a small space, as does the green summer foliage, which turns rosy red to scarlet in fall. This bush prefers sun, tolerates light shade and is easy to grow. Rabbits and mice will nibble it in winter, but otherwise it's pest- and disease-free.

□   *Forsythia*

Forsythia is moderately hardy but very robust and tolerant of city conditions. It produces a profusion of yellow flowers so brilliant that even I like them. It's a great candidate for early-spring blos-

□

While I was growing up in the relatively frigid wildernesses of northern British Columbia, one of the things that truly

som forcing. You should be sure to prune some of the old wood out at the roots after spring flowering.

□   *Hydrangea*

Hydrangeas come in a wide range of hardinesses and heights. All are easily propagated by cuttings and some by ground layering, so look around your neighbourhood for a free source. Mid-sized hills-of-snow hydrangea is covered in masses of pure white rounded flower clusters from midsummer to fall. The larger and woodier peegee hydrangea has conical flower clusters that open creamy white in late summer, gradually turning pink through the fall.

□   *Lilac*

No scent is quite like that of lilacs. They come in a wide range of colours, from white to deep purple, with clusters of single or double blossoms. Very hardy, lilacs tend to give back pretty much what you give them. They do best in neutral soil supplemented with peat moss or leaf mould. Removing old flower heads will encourage fuller bloom the next year.

□   *Mock Orange*

For two weeks in late spring, the mock orange produces irresistibly fragrant masses of single or double white flowers on arching, green-leafed branches. The bush thrives in full sun or partial shade and likes moist but well-drained soil.

□   *Sumac*

An extremely hardy, drought-resistant, sun-loving shrub often seen along roadsides and in wooded areas, the sumac makes a great landscaping addition to a small garden. It has bright orange or red fall foliage and ornamental fruits that persist into winter.

MY FATHER'S ROSE GARDEN

puzzled me was my father's courageous but essentially doomed 20-year attempt to grow roses in a climate that was much too harsh for them. I thought he was crazy at the time, but watching this epic and absurd struggle year after chilly year was an important part of my education as a gardener and as a human being. It taught me that growing living things is an essential activity and that being human involves a great deal more than hard-nosed pragmatism.

The lesson probably wouldn't have been quite so effective if my father hadn't been such a business-is-business pragmatist in every other way. Of the many things he tried to drum into my somewhat thick head, this was about the last thing he wanted to get through. But for all his chamber-of-commerce sensibleness, each spring he ordered new rosebushes and planted and nurtured them for the one or two blossoms they produced; each winter, the cold winds killed them. The next spring, he'd jerk the barren twigs from the ground and replace them with new roses.

What he was teaching me was that the human need for beauty is irrepressible. It was as irrepressible in him as in a concert pianist, and that is a truth about my fellow human beings I have never lost sight of, even though for many years, I had no idea where I'd learned it or from whom. It has taken me through some very dark and leafless days, in and out of the garden.

A few years after I left home, my parents retired and moved to the warmer climate of British Columbia's Okanagan Valley. One of my father's reasons for moving, I've long suspected, was that he could at last grow his beloved roses. For sure, one of the first things he did in his new place was to create a spectacular rose garden, one that he's enlarged and refined over the years.

Despite the lesson I learned because of them, roses aren't my cup of tea. Since they are my father's, I asked him to collaborate with me in writing the following section on growing roses.

Roses aren't difficult to grow if you have the right kind of climate and you observe some basic rules. They need full sun, fertilizing twice a year, a steady supply of water and a certain degree of isolation from other plants. If you can do it, a special area in the garden devoted to them is nice.

GROWING ROSES IN A COMPACT GARDEN

My father doesn't have any experience gardening in confined spaces, so his approach might seem a little different from what I've been preaching throughout this book. To my mind, rose gardening is very demanding and in effect dictates that a gardener with a small space is going to have to sacrifice a lot of other garden delights in order to be successful. Roses more or less demand monoculture, partly because the amount and kinds of insecticides required aren't compatible with vegetable growing and partly because roses really don't like any other kinds of plants. Rationally, this leaves small-space gardeners with some hard choices to make. In a very small gardening space, some gardeners say, it is an either-or choice — one ought to go strictly with roses or forgo the pleasure entirely. Going with roses alone is a viable choice. You can have an arresting display of blossoms throughout most of the season, and the fragrances will be truly remarkable. If your space is a little larger, you can do what one of my neighbours has done. His front yard is devoted exclusively to roses, while the back garden contains nothing but vegetables. All the other options involve either poisoning yourself or having a lot of sick or dead rosebushes littering the yard. Too bad gardening isn't a rational activity, eh?

PLANTING ROSES

Typical of the kind of horticulture that requires a long-term commitment, rose beds must be prepared well ahead of planting. If you're just starting out, prepare your beds in the fall for planting the following spring. If you can't do that, prepare the beds in spring, then wait for at least three weeks before planting.

WATERING ROSES

Roses don't like to be sprinkled. Sprinkling damages the blossoms and encourages mildew on the foliage. If you can afford it, use a permanent drip system made of half-inch plastic pipe equipped with a pressure reducer and a drip device set at the base of each rose. That will ensure a steady supply of moisture where and when it is needed. Otherwise, water very, very carefully, using either a soaker hose or a water-wand-equipped hose.

What every rose grower aspires to and few achieve: this arbour and white picket fence look as though they've been lifted right out of a book of fairy tales, but in the world of gardening, anything is possible. A place in the sun means these roses will bloom profusely and cast a little welcome cooling shade on the walkway.

When my father is planting new roses, he always digs an extra-large hole, about two feet deep and at least 18 inches across. In the bottom foot of the hole, he places a well-mixed combination of peat moss, steer manure and bonemeal. On top of that, he puts a few inches of rich topsoil, then fills the hole with water and lets it settle. Next, he tosses in some loose soil for the rose roots to straddle—so that the plant is high enough for the ultimate height of its crown to be four to five inches above the ground—places the rosebush in the hole and adds more topsoil. Then, with his foot, he settles the earth firmly around the plant so that it is level with the adjoining soil.

The safeguard of the extra-large hole and the nutrients ensure that the new rose will have access to a plentiful supply of food and drink as it develops.

They also enable it to develop an extra-strong root system.

□ ROSE PESTS AND DISEASES

Roses are susceptible to a large number of diseases and vulnerable to an equally large variety of insect attacks. The most common villains seem to be mildew and aphids. There is a range of products available to control these problems. Specific remedies are more effective than preemptive strikes, but I've seen my father mix two controls for spraying, usually a fungicide along with a powerful toxin like malathion. Some roses are more vulnerable to mildew than others, and he recommends avoiding the susceptible species or eliminating them as their weaknesses appear.

□ THE BASIC ROSE TYPES

About 10,000 varieties of roses are registered with the International Rose Registration Authority, and more than 1,000 are currently available in North America. Here is some general information about the basic types:

□ Wild Roses

A relative of the blackberry family, wild roses grow in many areas across North America. The flowers are five-petalled, pale to hot pink in colour and intensely and uniquely fragrant. They blossom for only a short period and are a little unruly for a small garden.

□ Old Garden Roses

Classes of roses that existed prior to 1867 (the year of the introduction of the first hybrid tea rose) fall into this broad category. Among them are the famous damask roses (a Middle Eastern — and therefore infidel — import that survived the religious madnesses of the Middle Ages within the walled monas-

The 'Showbiz' standard roses that flank this stone stairway are underplanted with Swiss chard, nasturtiums and heirloom petunias in a strategy that defies the author's advice to grow roses in their own area. Growing edible plants near roses precludes using some of the nastier chemical controls these temperamental flowers often require.

teries of Europe), moss roses, gallicas, albas, centifolias, China and tea roses. Most old roses have only one blooming period, which is early, abundant and spectacular. After that, there are only occasional repeaters. While the blossoms of the old roses make a definite statement, the form of each is less important than with the moderns.

□ *Modern Roses*

Most of the moderns bloom repeatedly and are more bushlike than the older shrubby roses. The easiest way to distinguish the three modern types is to look at their blooms and blooming characteristics.

□ *Floribundas*: Generally smaller, lower-growing plants than the hybrid teas, floribundas are therefore good for foreground planting. They are more floriferous, with multiple blooms at the end of a stem, but the blossoms tend to be smaller, although this difference is fading with recently introduced varieties.

□ *Grandifloras*: Larger and taller plants than either hybrid teas or floribundas, grandifloras are ideal as background in a compact garden. Like floribundas, they have sprays of blooms, but their blossoms are like those of hybrid teas.

□ *Hybrid tea roses*: The most perfect of roses, the hybrid teas were bred by crossing tea roses with smaller perpetual varieties. They produce blossoms singly through the season, one to a stem or occasionally in small clusters. Because the individual bloom form is so important, disbudding (side-bud removal), which allows the plant to pour all its energy into the main bud, is a good idea.

□ *Climbers and Ramblers*

Varieties of hybrid teas and floribundas have been bred to climb, but true climbers and ramblers can be distinguished by the fact that they bloom profusely just once a year. Climbers bloom in large clusters on old wood. Ramblers have more slender stalks, sparse foliage and clusters of small blossoms that ap-

pear once a year on new wood. Make sure you've got adequate space for them to do their rambling and climbing, or you'll regret it.

□ *Miniatures*

Commonly called fairy roses, these plants are rarely more than a foot tall and their blossoms are about an inch across. Not surprisingly, they're quite fragile and are more suitable for pots and wintering indoors than for setting out in the cold, cruel world.

□ *MY FATHER'S FAVOURITES*

It took me a long time to get my father to admit to favourites, because like most rose gardeners, he's so concerned that I understand the many evils that assail these plants. At first, all he'd say was that some rose varieties which had been problematic for him had given other gardeners little or no trouble even in the same climate. The success of a rose plant, he continued, seems to be governed by such factors as soil composition, elevation and wind, and every garden is different in those respects. For the longest time, I couldn't get him to talk about what he really does like, but eventually, he prefaced what he had to say about his likes and dislikes with a piece of advice. The advice is simple and very much in accord with the gardening philosophy of this book: be prepared to experiment, and be prepared to have some of your experiments go wrong.

Because he likes to examine and photograph blossoms, my father finally conceded that his favourite species are generally the hybrid tea roses. But he says floribundas have their place too — in hedges and other spots where a show of colour is slightly more important than the perfection of the individual blooms. He doesn't much like the grandifloras, which isn't surprising, given his particular interest in the shape and colour of individual flowers. And that was as specific as he would get.

He did point out that roses come in

93

practically all colours, reds predominating. For him, a large part of the delight of growing roses is the endless variety of different characteristics and colour combinations that one can choose from. Some roses, he said, have one colour on the upper side of the petals and another on the lower side. When you become interested in the culture of roses, he concluded, the satisfactions of exploring one's fancies are almost as limitless as the gradations from one rose to another. The more you find out, the more interesting it becomes. Colour is usually the most important consideration, but blossom size and shape, length of stem, special fragrances and even leaf colour and shape are other factors to focus on.

I told you he was a pragmatist.

THE ABSOLUTE PLEASURE OF VINES

I'm not quite sure why, but I'm so fond of vines that whatever I say here probably ought to be taken with just a grain of salt. I suspect that one reason I like them so much is that so few of them thrived where I grew up, and consequently, they seem like a luxury. But I also like vines because there are so many things they can do—and so many things you can do with them—in a compact garden. Vines are capable of astonishing feats of strength and cunning. They also produce some of the most elegant flowers, they can provide food, privacy and shade, and they have an amazing ability to make almost any unattractive structure look better than it should. Some of the most delicious garden aromas come from them, and they produce some of the most colourful autumn foliage.

Whole volumes have been written on vines, but I'll confine my discussion to the roles they can play in a small garden and to providing a few tips on how to care for them—and a few more tips on how to keep them from taking over. I'll divide them into annuals and perennials, because the two groups have rather different properties, present different problems and serve different garden functions.

PLANTING VINES

As with most plants, it's not a bad idea to overplant your vines, particularly the annuals and the smaller perennials. The perennials aren't difficult to move, and the cutting back that is part of the process is often rather good for them. In all my many transplantings, I've lost only a Hall's honeysuckle and several of the more fragile (and inexpensive) *jackmanii* clematises.

When you buy vines or are given them by a neighbour, find out what you can about their mature size and prepare beds for them much as you would for a shrub or a small tree. Because they travel, you can often plant them in a shady or unused area and train them to the spot where you want them. This may take a while, so don't hold your breath. The usual pattern with vines is that they're slow to establish, but once they're happily ensconced in a good spot, watch out. If you're planting a vine near the annual or vegetable garden, dig the root hole a little deeper than usual and line it with old metal flashings or roofing so that the roots don't invade the rest of the garden. This is particularly important if the vine is a robust one.

Wisterias cover the entire back end of my house, which happens to face south and gets a lot of sun during the summer. I've put the vines there for a purpose. One of them, a big, sun-loving Chinese wisteria, shades my study during the summer months. In winter, when its leaves are gone, it obligingly lets the light in. A few years ago, I planted a white Japanese wisteria across from it to cover the other side of the house. Slightly more fragrant than its Chinese cousin, it's a little less vigorous.

For a few years, I had a Virginia

The leaf stems of the clematis act as tendrils, curling around the support they are provided, so they do especially well when grown next to a fence, a slim tree or a trellis. As a rule, clematises tend to like neutral to alkaline soil, and this jackmanii *clematis will reward you with showy blossoms four to five inches across.*

creeper that ran 40 feet along the fence on the west side of the garden close to the house. It provided a real degree of privacy, but in the end, its roots became so invasive that it was starving everything around it. I tore it out and planted another in a more isolated spot, then trained it to climb a trellis along the narrow east yard between my house and the neighbour's. I trained the most fragrant of all the honeysuckles, a Hall's, to run up the railing of the back steps so that I could take in the rich scents as I walked out into the garden. When it was winter-killed, I replaced it with several species of clematis. They aren't fragrant, but they're hardier. To replace the lost honeysuckle perfume, I now keep potted nicotiana on the porch.

Depending on the orientation of your own garden, you can plant vines for whatever qualities you want: fragrance, size or seasonal blooms. Many vines are not very winter-hardy, so check with your neighbours or your local garden centre to find out which varieties are appropriate for your climate and other local conditions.

PERENNIAL VINES

There are no completely hardy perennial vines, so be careful with your choices. A once beautiful dead vine will break your heart.

Clematis

Clematises are not very hardy, so check to see whether you can grow them in your area. If they're marginal, try them anyway; they can be incredibly gratifying. Clematises have one basic peculiarity: none of them like to have their roots heated. Hence, I try to plant them in places where their roots can stay cool and sheltered. I've taken to planting rosemary about a foot away from them. The rosemary shelters the roots, and I suspect the two plants have a special affinity for one another, because everywhere I've done it, both plants go crazy. (I may be deluding myself here. Probably any number of plants could serve the same purpose.) If your climate can handle rosemary as a perennial, try the combination. I've suggested it to many friends, and they've all had the same results. I must add that if you live in a colder climate, you won't have much success with my favourites. Feel free to accuse me of malicious teasing.

Clematis montana rubens is the giant clematis, and it is my favourite. I had a huge one that eventually concealed most of one side of my house, and for

six weeks every spring, it was covered with 6,000 to 8,000 pale pink blossoms about 1½ inches across. It was killed by some early frosts several years back, so I replaced it with a hardier Japanese wisteria and planted another *C. montana* bordering on the alley. After only about four years, it has taken over most of the garage.

I know my description of *Clematis montana* sounds like an exaggeration, but it isn't. It is a very spectacular plant, and its vines can travel 40 feet without difficulty. This particular clematis flowers again late in the summer on new wood, although not nearly as profusely as the first time. There is a white variety, but it isn't quite as robust. Watch *montana*, because it tends to get ratty and can be very invasive. Cut it back in midsummer if you need to, but keep your pruning to a minimum otherwise. It's also messily deciduous and peculiarly susceptible to early winter frosts.

Clematis armandii is considered the evergreen clematis. It blossoms very early in the spring, and it is the only variety of clematis that carries much scent. It grows quite quickly and will go to 20 feet, but it's even more tender than the others, and a hard frost or high wind can easily damage it.

My favourite moderate-sized clematis is 'Bee's Jubilee.' It runs to 12 to 15 feet and produces numerous three-inch lavender blossoms throughout August and September. If you cut the flower heads off once they are finished, it will bloom more, as will most varieties. Except for cosmetic reasons, it really does not need to be pruned.

There is a host of other smaller clematises, many of which require hard pruning yearly. I like 'Niobe' and 'Rouge Cardinale' for their rich reddish purple blossoms, and some of my more ostentatious friends enjoy a variety called 'Horn of Plenty,' which produces enormous pale purple blossoms in early summer. I've got one of them, but I'm a little embarrassed by it.

☐ *Climbing Roses*

As I've suggested, I tend to stay off my father's gardening turf, and aside from his early career of planting things in snowbanks, he's always been the family expert when it comes to roses. Hence I have only one climbing rose in my garden, a white one. I kidnapped a shoot from a dying plant I found years ago in an abandoned garden on a nearby island. I planted it rather carelessly on the north side of my garage, where it is

One of the author's favourite vines, this Chinese wisteria depends upon the verandah columns and fascia for support as it climbs. Hardy or fragile, vines have a nonnegotiable requirement—something to climb. If gardeners don't provide one, most vines will find one on their own, whether it is an old tree stump, the remnants of a fence or another plant.

shaded by both the garage and the neighbour's lovely spring-blooming cherry tree and must compete for root space with some powerful *Hedera helix* ivy. Yet after only four or five years, the rose was shading the cherry tree and providing me with a second and more spectacular display of blossoms through most of June and early July. Unlike most roses, it is entirely disease-free, and it is apparently unconcerned about the ivy. A profuse supply of small white flowers emits a distinctly musty odour of which I've grown fond, although it isn't like that of any other rose I know. Since I don't know which variety it is and am pretty certain it's the only one of its kind on the planet, I can't pass its wonders on in any other way than to describe it to you. Does this sound like I'm teasing you again? Okay, sorry: 'Don Juan' is a vigorous and richly scented red climber you can obtain at any decent garden store.

◻ *Grapes, Hops and Other Fruit-Bearing Vines*

Across the alley along an unused patch of ground between one neighbour's garage and the next neighbour's fence, a hop vine battles all summer with a thicket of blackberries. This year, the hop vine seems to be winning. For those of you who have had to contend with wild blackberries, this anecdote will be self-explanatory, because almost nothing—human, chemical or otherwise—can defeat blackberries. Except, apparently, hops. You can also make beer with hops, I'm told, and it is not an unattractive vine.

More useful and considerably more productive in my neighbourhood are the grapevines I mentioned earlier. My Portuguese neighbours harvest immense amounts of excellent wine grapes each year, even though we do not have a climate that fosters good grapes of any kind. Usually the vines do well enough, and they're attractive, but our summers don't provide the heat grapes need to produce sugar. My neighbours get around this by training the vines onto structures that sit just above their garage roofs. The secret (although they giggle about it more readily than they'll talk about it) is the black asphalt shingles they've put on the roofs. These absorb heat during the day, radiate it back into the vines and hold heat well into the cool of the evening.

More and more people these days are planting kiwi vines, which are an import from New Zealand. They're sort of ugly, they're fragile, and you have to have two of them, a male and a female, in order to get any fruit. Gender detection is quite unreliable, and I've run across several gardeners who discovered to their dismay three or four years down the line that they had the Everly Brothers or two-thirds of the Andrews Sisters and had to start over. My advice is not to bother. They're not the best vine candidates for a compact garden anyway, and in a few years, kiwi fruit will have gone out of fashion.

◻ *Honeysuckle*

As you've no doubt figured out, I have a weakness for Hall's honeysuckle, which I think is the most fragrant member of the honeysuckle family. Many of my friends now have specimens of this variety, because they're easy to root. Good thing too, because they seem to die for the strangest reasons. I plant this honeysuckle close to doorways and gates—anyplace, in fact, where I'm likely to walk frequently or to sit, particularly in the evening when they are most fragrant. (Some people are far less enthusiastic about Hall's, claiming it has an offensive invasive habit, but that's not my experience.)

Wild honeysuckles grow across much of North America, and nearly all tend to be unruly. None of them, from the domestics to the natives, are twiners, and they are without suckers. Some will grow to 25 or 30 feet, but most varieties stay relatively small if not actually compact. They appear to dislike being pruned in the summer, and that can create housekeeping problems, because they sometimes get quite ratty.

☐ *Ivy*

In this group are some of the hardiest of vines. The evergreen *Hedera helix* makes both an aggressive climber and a ground cover. For both purposes, I prefer the smaller and more pinnate-leafed variety to the common one, although it is a little more susceptible to cold weather. Both will cover any unsightly wall, fence or stump in a short time, are self-supporting and require little or no care.

Ivy prefers shade, so it is useful for shady or northern exposures. If your winters are cold, use Baltic ivy, a slower-growing variety with leaves that are a brighter shade of green. Baltic ivy isn't quite so accomplished a climber, but it is actually more attractive and it is extremely hardy.

The two main deciduous ivies (related in that they belong to the same genus, *Parthenocissus*) are the famous Boston ivy and the Virginia creeper. Boston ivy has climbing suckers and requires no support other than a surface upon which to grow, while Virginia creepers are more variable. One variety of Virginia creeper climbs, but several don't, and none of them climb quite so prettily as Boston ivy. Where I live, they make up for that with their vigour, which exceeds that of Boston ivy. All of the deciduous varieties have gorgeous if somewhat short-lived autumn foliage.

☐ *Wisteria*

Wisteria is a wonderfully powerful sun-loving vine. If every house in North America had one, we'd all be better for it. Not only do the vines coil around anything and everything, but they produce long racemes of fragrant blossoms in late spring. This year, mine produced seedpods covered with an earth-green velvety cover that puts to shame any store-bought fabric I've ever seen.

Several varieties of wisteria display varying degrees of fragrance and blossom colour. The main distinction is between the Chinese and Japanese wisterias, of which the former coils counterclockwise, the latter clockwise. These plants are heavy feeders and require a lot of pruning. Prune them in the summer for shape (and control), and they'll bloom more heavily the following year. Take special care to provide strong and permanent support structures for these vines (mine bent a length of three-inch steel pipe enough that I had to cut the pipe to keep the plant from pulling either the fence or the house over). They are extremely heavy plants and, unlike most vines, don't like to be moved once settled.

☐ *ANNUAL VINES*

My friend Jim has convinced me of the pleasures of the domestic morning glory (very popular in the 1960s for nongardening reasons), of which 'Heavenly Blue' is a standard. Morning glories are strong climbers, but they're not in the same class as their wild cousins. Don't, whatever you do, make the fatal mistake of thinking that you can control wild morning glory. You can't, and if it finds its way into your garden, it is incredibly difficult to eradicate without dynamite and napalm, neither of which I can recommend.

I'm also a longtime fan of sweet peas, which come in a variety of bright colours. They like rich, manured soil and cool roots, and they require support. Use a net or string, because they won't hold to anything with a diameter bigger than half an inch. Stagger your plantings over time, but don't plant them too early in the season. They're easily grown from seed as bedding plants if you remember to nick the seeds with a sharp knife or razor blade or soak them overnight before planting. You can get a two- or three-week extension of the season this way. I don't buy them as commercial bedding plants, because for some reason, garden shops sell them only in mixed colours, and I like to stick with the blues and reds. Sweet peas are cheerily fragrant, and they're among the best of the cut flowers.

The cup-and-saucer vine amuses some people, and other annuals, such as the black-eyed Susan vine, aren't difficult to cultivate. But we shouldn't forget pole beans, which are ideal in compact gardens because they will out-produce any bush bean and can at the same time provide both privacy and aesthetic pleasure. Scarlet runner beans are my favourites, because they carry brilliant red blossoms. (For a discussion of pole beans, see pages 49-50 and 53.) Several of my neighbours train pumpkins, cucumbers or squashes as vines. One neighbour runs his pumpkin vines up over his porch and onto a heavy mesh trellis above his back door so that he can watch his pumpkins grow in the late summer and early fall. So far, no one has been injured by falling pumpkins, but I'm sure that one day soon, he'll get busted by the safety police.

Depending on your local climate, bougainvillea and several other fragrant small vines such as jasmine can be moved outdoors from the greenhouse or sunroom for the summer. In some places, tomatoes like the 'Sweet 100' and 'Sweet Million' cherry tomatoes can be turned into beautiful and productive annual vines. But those kinds of applications take an immense output of time and care. They are also a little out of the range of this book and of any climate I've gardened in.

PERENNIALS ARE FOREVER (SORT OF)

To be perennial means that you recur annually and indefinitely, as in "perennially shortsighted governments," "perennially greedy bankers" and "perennially optimistic dogs and gardeners." In the garden, the word has a slightly more technical meaning. Even though, strictly speaking, trees, shrubs and vines are perennials, they aren't what gardeners mean by the term. Garden perennials are those smaller garden plants that live more than two years. I guess we distinguish them from the larger permanent plants because they must have an optimism similar to that of gardeners to survive. They really should be called "persistents." Most of them die right back in the fall but, if they don't, spend the winter under a blanket of snow. You'd have to be obliviously optimistic to survive that kind of experience every year.

Whatever the reasons for their name, perennials, once they're in the garden, are theoretically there to stay. The really cooperative perennials stay the same size and shape year after year, coming up in the spring, flowering, then disappearing when the weather grows cold. I've heard of such perennials, but I've never actually seen one. Most perennials grow progressively larger as they grow older, by either multiplying or spreading.

All perennials require care and attention at the proper time and in the proper way. Some can be grown from seed, but that is often a hit-and-miss proposition. I prefer to obtain perennials as bedding plants at one of the local garden shops or from my neighbours. If you spot a plant you like in a neighbour's garden, mention how much you like it and how much you'd like one of your own. More often than not, your neighbour will appear at your back gate with one when the time is right for dividing plants.

PREPARING PERENNIAL BEDS

Most perennials don't like to be moved (although some insist on it every second or third year), so preparing a perennial bed well is important. Double-dig your soil, make sure it has adequate drainage (as far as I know, only cranberries like poorly drained soil), and make sure it has lots of humus. Try to design your perennial beds so that they allow you access without your having

to tramp on the soil. (Perennials don't like compacted soil.) If you can't do that, use squares of wood or paving tiles to step on. Obviously, these will need to be substantially larger than your shoe size. I found some one-foot-square paving tiles on a construction site a few years ago, and I've laid them in one of my larger perennial beds as permanent stepping-stones. It isn't a perfect solution, but short of a complete redesign

of the garden, they serve well enough. Don't go for walks in your perennial beds, and don't let children or animals do so either.

□ *PLANNING PERENNIAL BEDS*

Because perennials like to think they're going to be where you set them forever, it is particularly important to plan their beds with a lot of care. This is not to suggest that working with perennials is

Reliable perennials such as peonies, lilies and irises make this garden an easy-to-care-for space. The birch trees provide light shade, while the ivy on the house softens the line of the bricks and the window-box geraniums add colour.

ASHES TO CONCRETE

I know that D.H. Lawrence is out of fashion these days, but he was a great poet and a great lover of garden flowers, and I share his love of blue blossoms. Did you ever wonder where and how he got planted after he died? In some lovely English garden, surrounded by the flower species he most admired, right? That would be poetic justice, surely, given his grim coalmining origins in the British midlands and his lust for the natural world.

I'm afraid that poetic justice wasn't served. Anything but, as a matter of fact. After his death, Lawrence quickly became a cult figure, and his fans actually stole his ashes from his widow Frieda on several occasions. Frieda was famed for her strength of character and her persistence but not for her sensitivity to matters poetic. She managed to get the ashes back and eventually decided to fix the thieving fans—and Lawrence—permanently. His ashes, mixed in a block of concrete, form part of the cornerstone of a building somewhere in New Mexico.

like working with concrete. Planning carefully doesn't preclude being able to change your mind. But it does mean finding out how tall your prospective plantees are going to grow, how much they'll spread, when they'll bloom, in what colours, what their foliage is like and how they are going to interact aesthetically and ecologically with the plants around them.

A successful perennial bed is rather like a successful juggling act. You're trying, in a limited space, to do several complex things at once, and you're trying to draw attention to your successful moves, not your mistakes. It is best to remember that a successful juggling act isn't a 10-second display and that a juggler who gets all the pins in the air at once will shortly find them all on the ground at once. Does this sound impossibly complicated? It is sometimes. But there's no reason to become suicidal about it. In a compact garden, perennial display just can't be done the way it is in Rolling Acres. You simply don't have the same margin for error or the space to make big mistakes.

My solution? I improvise. I like to give my perennials quite a lot of room so that I can cultivate between them. In the extra space, I plant annuals that will provide floral display at times when perennials don't do much but sit there and look green—or old and straggly.

□   SOME FAVOURITE
                         PERENNIALS

I'm not a reliable source on perennials because, as you know, I prefer blue flowers. I'm also used to a range of choices that is narrowed by climate and light. Your selection will be limited too. At the end of this section is a listing of perennials, with information on light requirements, height, colour and flowering season. But I wouldn't have a garden without the following:

□   *Delphiniums*

Delphiniums are relatively hardy, and more important, because they come in

spectacular shades of blue, they are an obvious choice for me. They're available in attractive pinks and whites as well, if your tastes run to the garish. I prefer 'Pacific Giant,' which grows to five or six feet and needs support. It's a good choice for relatively inaccessible spots against a fence or wall. Smaller varieties are available, and they're equally pretty but less spectacular.

Cut your delphiniums back to the ground after they've flowered so that they don't exhaust themselves producing seedpods that generally don't seem to produce viable seed anyway. Cutting them back will also encourage a second bloom (albeit less reliable and showy than the first) late in the summer.

□   *Gentians*

I've tried to grow gentians ever since I read "Bavarian Gentians," the remarkable D.H. Lawrence poem. One of my sober-minded friends with a distaste for scrawny English poets informs me that Lawrence's gentians were actually downy gentians, a wildflower that is impossible to domesticate. This explains some of the difficulties I've had getting gentians to flower at Michaelmas (as in Lawrence's poem), but it deters me not at all. Gentians are small plants that produce one or two blossoms of the most gorgeous blue I've ever seen. The main problem I've had with them, whatever strain I happen to have gotten hold of, is that they die off every winter and don't come back the next spring. This has been going on for about 10 years, and I've spent an embarrassing amount of money buying new bedding plants without any improvement in my success rate.

□   *Irises*

A lot of people like irises. I really have no idea why. Bearded irises blossom for a very short period, their foliage looks like giant quack grass, the tubers spread and stick out of the ground, and the blossoms are, well, vulgar. I've noticed recently that the colours of some of the

more exotic varieties are almost decent, but I still think irises are what you'd get if cattle took up plant genetics.

That said, there are some wonderful exceptions, such as the beardless Siberian irises, which are hardy, disease-resistant and demand minimal attention. Breeders have added to their number and increased both their flowering season and colour range. Several of the dwarf varieties are nice, and the Japanese irises are very sweetly scented.

Almost every gardener finds an exotic perennial that seems specially designed to soothe his or her soul and soil. Botanical gardens are fine places to discover perennials, and a walk around the neighbourhood, if you look carefully, will also produce pleasant surprises.

☐ *Peonies*

As my father discovered to his delight, peonies will grow almost anywhere.

They're big, healthy-looking plants that flower spectacularly in whites, pinks and reds and have beautiful deep green leaves. Cut them back in the fall once their foliage has started to discolour and fade, and if your climate is harsh, give them some protective mulch. Friends claim that once settled, they are yours for life, but in my experience, they seem to have about a 6-to-10-year life span before one disease or another reduces their vigour. If you are planting them for the first time or transplanting them, be sure to place the growing tips (the reddish buds on the tubers) about two inches below the soil level. If they're exposed or too deep, they'll die or refuse outright to bloom.

☐ *Poppies*

The poppies that produce opium are supposedly illegal. They're also quite rare in North America. But the plants

An early-summer garden, with foxgloves, oxeye daisies and peonies all in bloom. In the background are lilies not yet in flower. The key to decorative gardening, as every beginner discovers, is engineering a perpetual display of colour, a feat more easily imagined than accomplished.

PERENNIALS

NAME	LIGHT	HEIGHT	FLOWER COLOUR	SEASON	SPECIAL NOTES
Artemisia	sun	low	silver-grey foliage	summer/fall	alternative to annual dusty miller
Baby's Breath	sun	tall	white	summer	alkaline soil; fills midborder holes; stake; dry soil
Bee Balm (Bergamot)	sun/shade	medium/tall	red, pink	summer	humus-rich, moist soil; well-ventilated; divide often
Bleeding Heart	sun/shade	medium	white, pink	spring	likes organic mulch; foliage dies back in summer
Columbine	sun/shade	medium	many	late spring	fertile, moist soil
Coral Bells	sun/shade	low/medium	white, pink, red	spring/summer	profits from being split every 3 years
Creeping Phlox	sun	low	pink, white, lavender	spring	3-to-4-week bloom; shear foliage after blooming
Day Lily	sun/shade	medium/tall	many	spring/fall	any soil; improves with age; multiplies
Hardy Geranium	sun/shade	medium	blue, pink, red	summer	easy to grow; any decent soil
Hosta (Plantain Lily)	shade	low/medium	insignificant	summer	well-drained, nitrogen-rich soil; slug-prone if damp
Peony	sun	medium	pink, red, white	late spring	appealing foliage; singles don't require staking
Pulmonaria (Lungwort)	light shade	low	pinkish blue	spring	almost any soil; leaves spotted white on green
Purple Coneflower	sun/shade	medium	pinkish purple	summer/fall	humus-rich, moist soil; keep out of midday sun
Sedum	sun	medium	pink	fall	good foliage; neat habit; hardy
Shasta Daisy	sun	medium	white	summer/fall	keep moist; hurt by freeze/thaw; divide every 2 years
Siberian Iris	sun/part shade	medium	blue, lavender, purple, white	late spring	moist, fertile soil; easy; hardy; good foliage
Spiderwort (Tradescantia)	sun/shade	medium	white, pink, purple	late spring	attractive foliage through summer

that most people think are opium poppies are really another related species called *Papaver orientale*, splendid plants which, once settled in a garden, produce vigorous, brilliant red blossoms in early to midsummer. They propagate both by seed and by root division.

Since you'd need about an acre of the true opium poppies to get high, forget about becoming a drug baron or even an addict. To keep the neighbourhood kids from vandalizing them, I tell everyone that mine are an Iranian variety which doesn't produce any opiate.

THE CARE AND FEEDING OF BULBS

Most bulbs provide spring blossoms and are planted in either the fall or early spring, depending on your climate. Summer bulbs, such as gladioli and fall crocuses, are a slightly different game and operate by different rules. There are several strict procedures to follow if you want to be successful with either kind, but the following are some general rules.

□ Survey the neighbourhood to see which varieties thrive there and in what conditions.

□ When you're purchasing bulbs at your local garden centre, pay close attention to whatever the intelligent-looking salesperson has to say about planting times and conditions. That might be more reliable than the printed material they give you, which frequently comes from another country and sometimes suffers from faulty translation.

□ Make an accurate map of where you plant your bulbs, and try to plant them in clusters or grids. They look nicer that way in a small garden, the arrangement won't cancel out your options for later plantings, and they'll be easier to locate when it is time for renovation.

□ If you can afford it, dig in a handful of bonemeal with new plantings. A sidedressing of 3-15-6 early in the spring will help keep your bulbs vigorous.

□ After the blossoms are finished, cut off the flower stalks, but don't chop the foliage immediately. When the foliage has died back so that it can be gently twisted by hand to disengage it from the bulb, it's ready to go. Bulbs need the green stuff to maintain health, even if they're eventually to be removed and stored through a cold winter.

□ If your bulbs can stay in the garden through the year, as can grape hyacinths and crocuses, make sure they're placed in spots that afford a certain degree of safety from being trod on and from oops-type cultivation.

□ Most daffodils are relatively permanent and trouble-free. Unfortunately, they're often yellow. Try to get the paler varieties if you can, and don't plant them in the shade unless you're willing to replace them every year or two. Crocuses, snowdrops and grape hyacinths can tolerate shade, but most bulbs don't like it. No bulb can stand soil that isn't well drained for very long.

□ Tulips have a limited life span in the garden: three years in rich, well-drained soil, two years if your soil conditions are less good. Every three years, I dig my tulips out in late summer, discard the small bulbs that have multiplied from the originals and let the healthy remainders dry out in a cool, dark spot for a month or so before replanting them along with new bulbs.

Squirrels seem to be especially fond of the flavour of tulips and will often dig them out and eat them. Short of shooting or poisoning the little monsters (which can get you into a lot of trouble), there's not much you can do about this. If you know where the squirrels nest, you can stop up the holes, but make sure you do this in mid- or late summer after the kits can fend for themselves. Don't block a hole until you're very sure that the nest is unoccupied. Whatever you do, don't feed the squirrels peanuts as a substitute. They'll dig up your tulips anyway, eat them and store the peanuts in the tulip bed.

BULLS

BULBS

NAME	LIGHT	HEIGHT	FLOWER COLOUR	SPECIAL NOTES
SPRING-FLOWERING BULBS				
Allium (Flowering Onion)	sun	low/medium	purple, red, yellow, white	late; many types; all good cut
Crocus	sun/ part shade	low	white, purple, yellow	very early; multiplies
Daffodil (Narcissus)	sun/ part shade	low/medium	yellow	plant in early fall; suitable for pots; multiplies; lasts longest where it is cool
Glory-of-the-Snow (Chionodoxa)	sun/ part shade	low	white, pink, blue	early; easily grown; foliage dies down quickly
Grape Hyacinth (Muscari)	sun/ part shade	low	blue, white	hardy; low-maintenance; long-lived
Hyacinth	sun	low	white, pink, blue, red	fragrant; easiest bulb to grow indoors in pots; bulbs diminish in size after 2 to 3 years
Snowdrop (Galanthus)	part shade	low	white	very early; good underplanting for shrubs, perennials
Squill (Scilla)	sun/ part shade	low	blue, white	Siberian hardier than Spanish
Tulip	sun/ part shade	low/medium	many	early, mid- and late-season varieties; good cut
SUMMER-FLOWERING BULBS				
Dahlia	sun	low/ medium/tall	many	good cut; blooms late summer to frost; enjoys sunshine and cool air (offer some shade in heat of day)
Gladiolus	sun	medium/tall	white, red, yellow, pink	plant every 10 days until midsummer for successive blooming; water deeply weekly; weed lightly
Lily (Lilium)	sun/ part shade	medium/tall	white, red, yellow, pink	plant in fall; well-drained soil; midway in bed; avoid root competition from trees, shrubs
Tuberous Begonia	part shade/ shade	low	red, orange, white, yellow, pink	rich, well-drained but moist, humusy soil; start indoors late winter or buy plants; continuous bloom all season; good potted or in hanging baskets

□ Good companion plants for bulb-rich beds are forget-me-nots and foxgloves. Both are biennials that reseed themselves if left alone. The blue forget-me-nots generally blossom about the same time as tulips and provide a lovely foliar and colour complement. Succeeding generations of forget-me-nots seem to become paler in colour, so I scatter a package of new seed in my bulb beds around midsummer every two or three years.

□ SUMMER BULBS

I grew up in a city of gladiolus freaks. The flowers were popular because they had the showiest blossoms that could survive the harsh climate. Gladioli remind me a little too much of irises, but they do have their uses, and they can be very pretty. Plant them (and other summer bulbs) in a sunny, well-drained location as soon as the soil is warm (successive plantings will extend the blooming season), and make sure you get them out again before the first frost. Without knocking the dirt off the bulbs or spraying them clean with the hose, tie the tops together, let them air-dry in a warm spot for a week or so, and store them in a cool, dark, dry spot until the next year.

Dahlias, which have about the same soil, sun and drainage requirements and provide a similar range of mostly vulgar colours, should be treated in exactly the same way as gladioli, even though they're tubers and not bulbs. They'll need to be stored differently, however. Fill a cardboard box with peat moss, place the washed and dried tubers in it, and store in the basement.

□ KEEPING PERENNIAL AND
BULB BEDS IN SHAPE

Keeping your flowerbeds in shape can be a tricky procedure, because you're often forced to choose between renewing the soil and trying to protect settled plants from disturbance. An inch of compost or well-rotted manure lightly dug into the soil in the fall along with a sprinkle of dolomitic lime will go a long way toward keeping your beds healthy. If a plant dies or if you replace some ageing bulbs, double-dig the soil and add lots of humus and fertilizer. Keep the bed weeded, but make sure you know which are weeds and which are self-seeding annuals like forget-me-nots. Never use a full-sized rake in a perennial bed. Don't use a backhoe either. Try a long-handled cultivator, the smaller the better.

□ THE FLEXIBILITY OF ANNUALS

Annuals are plants that germinate, blossom, reproduce and die in a single season. They can grow as large as some perennials do, but as a rule, the larger the plant is intended to be, the later in the year it will bloom. Those whose seeds were planted early indoors in pots and then transplanted into the garden may be in bloom by May, but don't expect annuals that have been started by direct sowing in the flower garden to bloom until after midsummer.

What this means, in practical terms, is that if you want annuals to bloom before then, they've got to be tricked into it. Cool-weather-loving pansies are the most common example. In warmer

climes, they are started from seed in the summer (or bought as bedding plants in the fall) and blossom during the late spring and early summer after a season of cold. In a colder climate, pansies are among the first annuals one starts from seed. I start mine around the first of January along with my onions. (Biennial forget-me-nots, which self-sow, do the trick on their own. They germinate one year and flower the next.)

There's another trick with annuals. Since the purpose of a plant's life is to set seed and thus reproduce, which it will do once it has flowered, we have to fool it into thinking it hasn't accomplished its life's work yet. We do this by

ANNUALS

NAME	LIGHT	HEIGHT	FLOWER COLOUR	SPECIAL NOTES
Ageratum	sun/shade	low	blue	easily sown in flats; good edging plant
Alyssum	sun	low	white, pink, purple	fragrant; cool-temperature bloomer; hardy; self-sows
Aster	sun	medium/tall	many	good cut; direct sow; tolerates mild frost
Browallia	shade	low	blue	winter houseplant; easily seeded in flats
Coleus	shade	low	insignificant	foliage is patterned green/red/white/maroon
Cosmos	sun	tall	white, pink, red	self-sows if undisturbed; good cut
Forget-Me-Not	shade	low	blue	biennial; can be invasive through prodigious self-sowing
Foxglove	sun	tall	many	requires staking; most are biennial
Geranium	sun	low/medium	white, pink, salmon, red	winter houseplant; cuttings root; trailing/scented varieties
Impatiens	shade	low/medium	white, pink, purple, red	continuous flowering; no dead-heading; winter houseplant
Lobelia	shade	low	blue, magenta, lilac, white	good in containers; cool-temperature bloomer
Mallow	sun	medium/tall	pink	direct seed
Nasturtium	sun	low/medium	orange, yellow, white, pink	edible; cool-temperature bloomer, even in poor soil
Nicotiana	sun/shade	medium	white, pink, red	scented; evening-flowering
Pansy	shade	low	purple, blue, maroon, yellow	good in small bouquets
Petunia	sun	low	many	good in containers; fragrant
Poppy	sun	medium	white, pink, red	direct seed; self-sows; does not cut/transplant well
Snapdragon	sun	low/medium	many	good cut flower; best in cool weather
Sweet William	sun/shade	low	white, pink, red, purple	biennial
Wax Begonia	shade	low	pink, white, red	winter houseplant; root cuttings
Zinnia	sun	low/tall	many	direct seed; tolerates mild frost; good cut

dead-heading—removing the dead flower heads. Another thing: those flats of madly blossoming annuals you see in early spring at the garden centre are filled with plants that have been forced to bloom in the greenhouse. When you transplant them into your own garden, it's a good idea to cut them back right away to encourage root growth, give them a better shape and cause them to produce more flowers.

A lot of plants that we think of as annuals are actually biennials. This is particularly true in the vegetable garden, where most of the root crops (carrots, beets, parsnips and most onions) are biennial. We simply harvest them at the end of the first year. If left to themselves, they will flower and produce seed in the second. It is less common in the annual flower garden, but it happens, as with forget-me-nots.

Lots of annual flowers are relatively easy to grow. You simply pop the seeds into the garden, and up they come, as with cosmos, sweet peas and others. You can extend their season by starting them under growing lights or by purchasing them as bedding plants from your local garden shop. If you're growing your own, make sure you check the seed packet's recommended outdoor planting time. Many annuals have been brought here from the tropics, which means they have to be germinated artificially, often under special and tricky conditions. Again, you can start them indoors yourself or buy commercial bedding plants that have been started in greenhouses.

Generally speaking, I'd advise beginners to buy bedding plants until they are ready to deal with the vicissitudes of starting their own flowers from seed. If and when you do start your own, remember that seed companies frequently underestimate the difficulties of germinating plants from seed. If the package instructions are very specific, problems may be ahead, and you'll do well to follow the suggested procedures with extra attention. I've been trying to germinate a species of blue poppy for about eight years now, without success—and at $2 a package. I'm convinced that this particular poppy can be germinated successfully only by geniuses in a space shuttle, but I'm still trying (and with the full knowledge that poppies are not receptive to being transplanted).

Of course, some of my friends and neighbours have had successes, and so have I. I've grown browallia from seed where others have failed, and I've been

One could only describe this garden as that of a serious decorative gardener—or at least one who knows how to take advantage of available space. From hanging baskets of annuals, flowering hydrangeas and trellised clematises to lobelia, pansies, alyssum and dahlias, this garden has most of the bases covered.

DISPLAY TACTICS

Provided that you remember a few basic rules, planning for a display of annual flowers takes no special skills.
□ *Make a plan of what you'd like to have happen, and try to stick with it. Success won't come all at once, but after a couple of years, you're sure to get the hang of it. Keep track of your plans so that in succeeding years, you'll remember what did well and what did not.*
□ *Remember that tiny plants can grow very large, and don't crowd your seedlings. This is hard for a beginner to remember at first, but if you overcrowd a plant, it won't thrive. If you sow directly into the garden, be prepared to thin the seedlings just as you would in the vegetable garden.*
□ *Annuals and perennials can happily coexist, although it will take some care in a compact space. The trick is to remember not to do too much.*
□ *As always, pay attention to the light and drainage requirements of what you intend to plant.*

starting my own petunia seedlings for years. My friend Jim has had startling success collecting seed from his petunias, which he does as much to track the genetic alterations that occur as out of any wish to save money.

In general, though, beginners are more familiar with unpleasant surprises than with successes, which you'll discover the first time you open an annual seed package, decide that the company sent you an empty one by mistake and shake the nearly microscopic seeds all over the kitchen table.

□ ### BLOSSOMS THROUGHOUT THE SEASON

A full season of blossoms is every gardener's fantasy. It is possible in a compact garden, but quite frankly, it is very difficult to achieve, so give yourself a break. I've moved increasingly toward monocultural plantings that are spectacular for a part of the season, and I've learned to compensate for the periods when parts of my flower garden are less than prime by spotting the temporarily dull zones with potted plants. Use clay pots, and bury them in the soil a quarter to halfway. Clay looks nicer and it isn't plastic. Ten-inch (no. 22) pots are best—they hold an adequate volume of soil, and they aren't too heavy to move around. At the end of the season, the outsides of the pots will be a bit discoloured, but they're easily cleaned, and in my view, the stains will simply add character—something you won't ever achieve with a plastic pot.

Another option is to attempt spectacular displays of colour that will draw attention for a short time. You can achieve this either with one or two species (such as sweet peas and asters) in a riot of different colours or with a display of one type of flower in slightly different shades of the same colour (provided it isn't yellow). This summer when I visited Toronto, I saw a small yard that had no flowers in it except a 5-by-30-foot border of cosmos, and it was very striking. Another alternative

is to add a border of plants with attractive or interesting foliage that lasts throughout the season. Dusty miller, which has very pretty silver-green foliage, is a good example.

In some cases, you can make two gardens of one: a pansy display will last until midsummer, and as the plants start to fade, replace them with pot chrysanthemums and other species that will carry through to early or midfall. (Chrysanthemums are actually perennials, but the nurseries grow them in such hyperactive conditions that they almost never survive the winter, even in Vancouver's mild climate.) Talk to staff at your local garden shop about which plants are best for your area.

□ ### SOME FAVOURITE ANNUALS

In a compact garden, you have to be resourceful with annual flowers. My advice is to please yourself and make it interesting. That's always easier than achieving *House Beautiful* standards and is much less stressful. By the way, annuals have an important and sometimes underemphasized advantage: if you make a choice that you wind up hating, you can make sure it never enjoys a spot in your garden again.

□ #### Cosmos

This tall annual is an attractive plant while it is growing, and the blossom display can be quite splendid. It's good as a background or border plant, and I've known several people who grew huge patches of it. Cosmos come in a variety of colours, from white to a hot pink that borders on purple, and are particularly attractive when integrated with sweet peas and lavatera, none of which come in yellow, as far as I know.

□ #### Geraniums and Petunias

I've grouped these together because they're both best as potted plants. Petunias are slightly fragrant, and there are also scented geraniums with some very exotic aromas. Don't try to grow petunias from seed until you've got some experience with the art of starting seeds—and good equipment. The scented geraniums blossom much less profusely than the common varieties, and they're generally less vigorous. Geraniums aren't difficult to winter over indoors, and one can take cuttings from them in the late summer for planting the next year.

◻   *Marigolds*

I detest marigolds. They're ugly, they come only in unattractive yellows and oranges, and they stink. A lot of people seem to like them, and otherwise reliable experts make all kinds of ridiculous claims about how they scare away bugs and communists. Well, so do pesticides, pit bulls and nuclear weapons, which are about as welcome in my garden as marigolds. My friend Jim had a pleasant experience with them, though. He grew a batch of about 20 plants from seed, put them out in the garden, and within three days, the entire bunch was mowed down by slugs. Interestingly, the slugs didn't touch anything else in the vicinity. I suggested to Jim that this was probably because they crawled off and died of disgust.

◻   *Nicotiana*

Lately, I've grown increasingly fond of this vigorous annual, which is supposedly a relative of cigarettes and cigars. It seems to like partial shade as much as full sun (flowering best in low-light conditions), doesn't mind being potted and will self-sow profusely. Best of all, nicotiana is night-scented, and around dusk and for several hours afterward, the flowers will fill the garden with their particularly sweet aroma—which isn't at all like that of cigarettes. The best choice for fragrance is 'White,' although it isn't the prettiest one because its blossoms are really a very pale green. The deep purple 'Nicki Red' strain is much more compelling and, when planted with 'White,' will self-sow in succeeding years, producing flowers with stronger scent and white, pink and deep purple petals. The hybrids are shorter and more compact and come in a wide range of colours. They are also sometimes more heat-tolerant than the older varieties and are therefore more suitable for small containers in full sun. Unfortunately, they are not nearly as fragrant as the nonhybrids.

◻   *Poppies*

Many fine annual poppies exist, most of which will self-sow; some are much more difficult to grow than others. The most robust ones seem to be yellow and orange, so take care. The 'Fairy Wing' poppy, a recent addition from Europe, self-sows relatively well, is extraordinarily pretty and comes in a diaphanous white. I recommend it, but the seeds are sometimes hard to find.

THE CUTTING GARDEN

As you've probably figured out, I think the best flowers for cutting are other people's. You can obtain them in relative safety by pruning whatever you see sticking through the fences in back alleys at night, and you can often acquire them legally by sticking your face into a neighbour's garden, mooning over how much you like the flowers and looking needy.

Flowering shrubs are excellent targets for either of the above methods in early spring. These include forsythia, which, as you know, is the only yellow blossom I'm fond of, probably because it is among the year's first and the yellow is so brilliant. Lilacs and roses don't mind pruning, nor do asters, sweet Williams, zinnias, chrysanthemums, geraniums, Michaelmas (blue) daisies, cosmos, pansies, sweet peas, forget-me-nots and foxgloves. Any of the bulbs will do well as cut flowers, although in my opinion, bulb flowers ought to stay in the garden. Poppies don't like being cut and will wilt within hours, as will petunias and lavatera. A bouquet of marigold blossoms is particularly attractive—at the bottom of a garbage can.

A NOTE ON SHADY GARDENS

◻

If you're cursed with having a portion of your garden in total shade (a complete absence of direct sunlight), it is probably located in your basement, and about all you're going to be able to grow there without growing lights is fungus. You can lift the curse by opening the door and strolling outside, where the worst thing you'll have to deal with is deep shade. What I'm trying to say, in my roundabout way, is that into almost every garden at least a little light falls. The problems of shady garden spaces are quite real, but they're seldom life-threatening, and there are usually solutions.

One of the most important skills required is an ability to decipher the terms used on seed packages and in gardening manuals. "Shade" means that an area receives less than three hours of direct sunlight daily, "partial shade" means three to five hours, "partial sun" means five to seven hours, and "full sun" means more than seven hours of sunlight daily.

All of these terms, however, assume that it is always a sunny day, a condition that occurs only in parts of the Sahara and Walt Disney's social planning manual. If you live in an area where overcast skies or rain clouds are frequent visitors, you'll have to make a slight adjustment to compensate, but in the vast majority of climates, "shade" means less than five hours of direct sunlight a day. If part of your garden space experiences those conditions, you'll have to exercise care. Most plants, particularly flowering ones, require at least moderate doses of direct sunlight.

I have some fairly radical notions about what to do in deep-shade areas, which I'll offer along with a caveat: if your garden is truly shaded, it's worth looking at a gardening book that devotes itself specifically to the problem. All I can do here is give you some basic advice about dealing with shade and a few tips from my own experience.

My first recommendation is that you shouldn't try to have a lawn in a shaded area. What you'll end up with is a lawn that has a lot more moss—or weeds—than grass. Actually, I'm no fan of any kind of lawn in a small garden, partly because the environmental requirements of grass are so different from those of most other plants and partly because I hate mowing grass. Shaded lawns are the worst kind of lawn. To keep them looking decent, you will have to use all kinds of horrible chemicals to control the moss and weeds. If your area is small enough, I'd suggest replacing the grass with a combination of raised beds and patios of concrete or clay tiles. If the area is larger, use trailing ground covers – do anything short of parking cars on it.

As luck would have it, a fairly large number of plants will tolerate shade, and a few won't put up with direct sun at all. The species that will thrive in your area will, however, be governed by other local parameters such as climate, drainage and soil composition.

For obvious reasons, most ground-

cover species are shade-tolerant, and many actually prefer it. Periwinkles and ivies demand shade, as do hostas and lilies-of-the-valley. Likewise, hydrangea bushes thrive in the shade, as do some of the azaleas.

I am no enemy of shade because, as it happens, my favourite flowering plant, lobelia, is a shade lover. 'Crystal Palace' is a compact, deep blue border or pot annual, while 'Sapphire' is a splendid trailer with white-centred blue blossoms. Pansies also tolerate shade and will actually last longer in a shady spot because they're away from the heat they dislike. Begonias, which come in a range of colours, positively detest direct sun, as do coleus and most members of the impatiens family.

A final tip before you consult a more intensive text on the science of shade gardening: shade does not have to be a permanent feature. I have a friend who recently bought a tall, narrow Victorian house in Toronto with a long, narrow backyard that was shady and overgrown. She hired a professional tree-care outfit to trim back some of the branches of the trees that bordered her yard, and before her eyes, her garden space was transformed into a largely sunny spot with a few shady areas.

Not all plants are sun lovers, which is just as well, given the gardens some of us inherit. These three plants—coleus, white impatiens and purple browallia—are ideal for the shade garden, providing interesting foliage and flowers.

You should also remember that as your garden—and your neighbour-hood—matures, available light is going to change. When another friend bought her house, the yard was in full sunlight. Nearly five years later, the Manitoba maples that line the eastern boundary of her property have grown substan-

□

It's a surprisingly short jump from the kind of gardening techniques I use in a small space to the strategies one must employ in a condominium or apart-ment-balcony environment. The chief differences are in the amount of avail-able garden space and in the lack of ac-cess to ground soil. The problems you'll face aren't exactly the same, but they are similar, differing mainly in scale and degree. There are usually problems with light—either too much or too little—or with moisture and wind—again, too much or too little. It might be helpful to think of the raised beds in my small-lot garden as something like large, bottomless containers.

□   POT PREPARATION

If you live in a place with a closed or open patio but no ground soil, you can garden very successfully in containers by following a few basic rules.

Make sure your containers are deep enough for adequate soil. You'll need a minimum soil depth of 12 inches, al-though 18 inches is better—even more if you plan to plant trees in the con-tainers. You will also need good drain-age. Remember that containers will need at least two inches of porous ma-terials on the bottom. You can use gravel, potshards or, if your containers are large and need to be moved around, concrete pumice (available at building-supply shops). If your containers are made of wood, make sure that there is an airspace between them and the floor or the ground and that they have holes in the bottom to let out excess water. Using wood that is at least two inches

tially (these trees seem to grow about 12 feet a year). Over the next several years, my friend's yard will be in shade for significant parts of the day. She will have to choose her permanent plant-ings with some foresight, keeping in mind that shade lovers will get happier and happier there as the years pass.

CONTAINER GARDENING

thick, assemble the containers with gal-vanized nails or, better, galvanized wood screws. Pressure-treated wood is preferred because any other kind will last no more than two or three years, even if the containers are lined with plastic. Cedar will do, but it really doesn't last much longer than other un-treated woods—five years at most. Don't use plywood or particleboard for containers. A little moisture will soon transform plywood into separate (and very warped) sheets of veneer, and it will turn your particleboard into saw-dust. Prefabricated concrete containers are fine, provided they come with holes in the bottom for proper drainage. They're expensive and very heavy to move, so think twice before using them on a balcony.

If your gardening space is on a deck or balcony, the rule of thumb is this: don't plant anything in a container that you would be unable to lift once it is full of soil. Anything heavier will have an effect on the deck that you or your landlord won't like—and it will have that effect astonishingly soon. There's nothing very mysterious about this. A 200-pound man standing on a deck or balcony for two years without moving would make 9 decks out of 10 collapse. I'm sure you get the point, so don't try this experiment at home, folks.

I'm a great believer in terra-cotta pots. Relatively inexpensive, they are long-lasting if treated properly, and they grow more attractive with age. They can be moved more easily and safely than square wooden containers of equivalent volume. Large ceramic pots

While the author's colour of preference is blue, this gardener has concentrated on a garden mostly of greens and whites that includes shade-loving hostas, variegated leaves and a variety of pale flowers.

are fine too, but they're generally more expensive. As for plastic pots, I have to say again that I don't like them. They're usually somewhat cheaper and lighter than other pots, but plastic wears out rather quickly when exposed to sunlight, and quite frankly, it looks like plastic – new plastic when it's new and old plastic after one or two seasons. (I've also noticed that thieves prefer large plastic pots to terra cotta. This seems to confirm my longtime theory that crime and bad taste go together.)

The drawback to terra-cotta pots is that they suck moisture out of the soil when in direct sunlight, so plants tend to dry out more quickly than in ceramic or plastic pots. If you paint the insides of the pots with silicone sealer, varnish or Varathane, you can avoid this.

One rule I try to abide by when I'm planting in outdoor pots is never to use a pot smaller than 10 inches across the

mouth if it is going to be subjected to direct sunlight. Those in full shade can be quite a bit smaller. I also use plates with high lips under the pots to retain water. Clay saucers are now often treated to reduce moisture loss.

☐   *Soil for Containers and Pots*

Buying potting soil for large outdoor pots can be expensive, and I generally don't like the commercial mixes, which often are little more than heavy garden soil or peat mixed with manure. This type of mix usually has too much nitrogen in it – which means there will be too much green growth. I've learned, instead, to mix my own soil in a large plastic garbage can. I use two shovelfuls of garden soil, two of mushroom or steer manure, one of fine peat moss and one of construction sand. Into that, I toss a handful of 6-8-6 fertilizer and, because my soil is acidic, a handful of

dolomitic lime. If I know that the pot is going to be in a particularly hot spot, I toss in one shovelful of vermiculite, which is an additive that holds moisture. I'm never very exact with these proportions, and I don't think you need to be. After a while, you'll get the hang of it and settle on the ratios that work best for your locale.

□ SOME POTTED PLANTS FOR SUNNY LOCATIONS

Geraniums and petunias are ideal as potted plants for sunny locations. They both come in a wide range of colours and characteristics, including trailing versions, if you like plants in hanging baskets. I don't, because it's hard to get a hanging basket that isn't made of plastic, and besides, I always end up pouring cold water down the front of my shirt when I water them. Sphagnum-moss-lined hanging baskets are very

pretty, but they're a nightmare to keep watered and shouldn't be considered for sunny spots. I've experimented with them a lot—using bottom trays to hold water or soil-filled plastic-bag inserts. Both worked reasonably well but not in full-sun locations. If you use a plastic-bag insert, make sure you punch enough holes in it that your moss won't die from lack of moisture. (A final comment: if someone were to invent an attractive, functional container for hanging plants, they'd make a fortune.)

□ SOME POTTED PLANTS FOR SHADY LOCATIONS

You already know that my favourite annual for shady locations is lobelia. It also happens to be a perfect plant for pots. I prefer the blues, but lobelia is also available in attractive reds and whites. I've noted that begonias are shade lovers and that they like to be

Gardening doesn't have to be just a ground-level activity. Urban dwellers are increasingly taking advantage of any and all available space. This rooftop garden features a wooden arbour that provides support for both hoses and vines and creates shade while the planters position canna lilies in the sun.

DECKS AND BALCONIES

If you're gardening on a sun deck or an apartment balcony, you'd best begin with an inventory of the amount of sun and wind you receive, because both determine what you'll be able to grow and how much care you'll have to take. If you have an abundance of both, use larger pots, and be sure to add lots of vermiculite to the potting soil: this will keep the weight down and help conserve moisture. On hot, sunny days, you'll have to water both morning and evening. But the choice of what you can grow is limited mainly by your diligence and imagination, and your success will be determined mainly by your memory. If you forget to water for two or three days, it'll all be over. Balcony gardens don't take summer vacations, and they don't like it when you do.

grown in pots. Tuberous begonias are particularly suitable for hanging containers. Nicotiana also does well in pots of sufficient size, and because of its sweet scent, I recommend it for doorways and any spot where you sit outside in the evening.

Even though they don't flower very spectacularly, I prefer the scented geraniums to the more common varieties for potted plants. I like to keep several scented geraniums next to my favourite balcony chair so that I can crinkle their aromatic leaves. Regular geraniums come in a wide variety of pleasant colours, none of which are yellow or orange. Petunias don't come in yellows either, although the plant geneticists have taken to producing them in some very silly variegated combinations with bizarre names. I prefer the Cascade strain, which seems to blossom longer and more vigorously than the other kinds. By the way, spent blossoms should be pinched off as soon as possible, particularly with petunias. As mentioned earlier, this practice will speed the development of new blossoms.

□   *GROWING VEGETABLES IN CONTAINERS AND POTS*

You can grow vegetables in containers with surprising ease if you stick to some basic rules.
□ Make sure your containers are deep enough (18 inches minimum) and the soil is rich. Be sure to give the plants a steady, moderate supply of water.

□ Stick to the varieties adapted to containers—patio or subarctic tomatoes, peppers, radishes, bush cucumbers, squashes, miniature carrots and designer lettuces. Don't try to grow corn, beans or peas in containers. In my experience, they just don't take to it. Incidentally, patio tomatoes look cute, but they're sort of tasteless.
□ Most herbs, particularly the annuals, do well in pots and containers.

□   *SUMMERING YOUR INDOOR PLANTS*

Most of your indoor plants will like it if you place them outdoors in fine weather, and many of them will find it downright invigorating. Not surprisingly, they seem to prefer sheltered locations with dappled or indirect light rather than full sun, which will burn many of them. If you are so inclined, you might build tiered shelving in an unused part of your yard to house these plants over the summer (although if your garden is regularly subjected to strong winds, you may not want to do this). Even cactuses like being outdoors in good weather, but they seem to like direct sun even less than most other indoor plants do.

Remember to spray indoor plants that you have placed outside with a solution of 5 percent diazinon a couple of days before you bring them back in for the winter, or they're likely to sprout massive and devastating insect infestations a few weeks later.

□   GREENHOUSES AND SIX-MIL PLASTIC

About two years ago, I came within a hair of buying a greenhouse. When it came time to make the decision, I sat down and calculated the amount of money involved, both the purchase price and the operating costs. I talked with a couple of friends who had already taken the plunge, and I heard complaints and stories of disasters. In my opinion, greenhouses are inevitably hard to heat in fall, winter and

spring and equally tricky to ventilate properly in summer. They are also expensive catchalls for exotic plant diseases, excellent breeding grounds for insect pests and superb targets—intentional or otherwise—for flying objects. Much as I liked the idea of growing all my own bedding plants in elegant surroundings and enjoyed dreaming of jasmines and bougainvilleas, I decided that buying a greenhouse wasn't worth either the emotional or the material expense. A single glance at the haggard and careworn faces of my greenhouse-owning friends was enough to convince me. I began to look around for more practical alternatives, and I must have looked for at least five seconds before discovering six-mil plastic.

For anyone who gardens in an uncertain climate, six-mil plastic is the greatest thing since sliced bread. It can do more things in your garden than a greenhouse can. It can even do what a greenhouse is supposed to do. It is portable, flexible and reusable. It is also cheap, particularly if you buy it by the roll or half roll or are willing to cruise construction sites for abandoned sheets. I use it for cold frames, cloches, frost shelters, soil warmers and dryers and even for semipermanent windbreaks that stay in place right through the season. When its particular application is finished, I take it off the frames, roll it up and store it in the garage. It isn't quite as pretty as greenhouse glass, but it is wonderful stuff. (I recommend the six-mil weight. Anything lighter is too flimsy, and heavier plastics, if you can get them, tend to be too opaque. Heavier plastic will also crush your plants if the wind tears it from the frame.)

You don't have to be a carpenter to handle the plastic well either. In fact, if you're like me—leaning well to the amateur side when it comes to carpentry—it's a real advantage if you're not. I slap together makeshift structures with whatever loose boards I can find and then staple the plastic on with a staple gun. The structures aren't symmetrical, and they aren't airtight, which is just fine, because ventilation is required. If the wind tears a corner loose, I just staple it back the next day. All you need to take these structures down once you're done with them are a few well-aimed swings of a hammer. Unlike greenhouses, such structures give rise to neither paranoia about vandals and acts of God nor the need for an investment banker.

I like six-mil plastic because it challenges my creativity. I've found a number of highly successful and novel uses for it. Earlier (on pages 65 and 70), I described how it helps boost the yield of my tomato and basil crops. Here are some additional ideas: I leave my tomato tent frame in place all summer to protect the lowest clusters of tomatoes from cold winds, which I think helps them to mature a little earlier. Along the lower edge of the tent frame, I leave an 18-inch strip of plastic. When cold or wet weather comes sooner than expected, I simply restaple the plastic to the frame and let the tomatoes ripen inside. I've also used makeshift plastic tents to help squashes and cucumbers get a better start, to keep lettuce, spinach and corn salad going well after the first frosts and to wrap tender perennials during cold snaps. I'm sure you'll discover your own unique applications.

□ A NOTE ON COLD FRAMES
AND CLOCHES

Cold frames are useful devices, particularly in colder regions. My objection to them is that they are complicated, often expensive to build and usually can't be moved without a major production. In a small garden, they can mean a significant loss of productive garden space or storage problems. Old windows, if you can get hold of them, can cut the material cost of cold frames significantly. I've got some, and I use them in combination with—surprise—six-mil plastic to construct temporary cold frames for early spring plantings.

When you're building cold frames and cloches (which are sun or rain caps that protect your plants), keep in mind the extremities of weather they might have to face. If you live in an area that experiences late-spring snowfalls, increase the angle of the glass or plastic accordingly so that the weight of wet snow doesn't break through.

A wide variety of commercial cloches is available today. Unfortunately, most of them are either expensive or compli-

The tiny yellow flowers are not yet out on the Russian olive tree, but this backyard patio gets all the colour it needs from containers of flowering tulips and hyacinths. The raised beds also hold permanent plantings of evergreen shrubs.

cated to assemble. If you're using a commercial cloche costing $1.50 to shelter a young tomato or squash plant, for instance, you're paying too much. The clear plastic bags you get free from the supermarket will often do the same trick—just vent the top of the bag, and remember to remove it before you go to work each morning if bright sun is forecast. If you're not rich, these kinds of considerations are important. Remember to improvise.

STARTING PLANTS INDOORS

Is it really worthwhile to start your own garden plants from seed indoors? For beginners, the sensible answer is no. It is a lot of trouble, terrible things can and will happen, and you will become very discouraged. Most of what you want is more easily obtained at your local garden centre. The plants you buy there will be healthier and happier than you can make them, and they really don't cost that much.

Everything I just wrote is perfectly true, and prudent beginners will take it to heart and act accordingly. But "prudent beginners," when it comes to gardening, is an oxymoron, and anyway, a deeper wisdom is likely to prevail in this matter. You'll want to grow your own, and there are good if not wholly rational reasons why this is so.

For starters, most nurseries grow only plant species and varieties that are common and easy to sell, which means the selection is usually limited. Sooner or later, you'll find yourself with a list of plants you absolutely must have in your garden. Another slightly more mystical reason is that there is something wonderful about starting plants from tiny seeds and something almost irresistible about doing it successfully.

But beware. Waiting for you is a virtual cesspool of half-truths, overly optimistic and unintentional misinformation and some outright lies.

Don't start seeds on a windowsill. It never works—unless you're willing to set up a cot and sleep next to them. If your seeds do germinate, you'll have placed the young plants in the botanical equivalent of hell—insufficient light, cold coming from one side and heat from the other, animals tramping on them and clumsy, forgetful humans accidentally elbowing them onto the floor. They may even experience what cats like to do in trays. If windowsill-bred plants ever make it to the garden, they are almost certainly going to be neurotic. Flowers will come out the wrong colour, tomatoes the wrong size, and almost all, once they're in the garden, will sit there and do nothing for a long time while they recover from their cruel childhood.

What I'm suggesting is that raising plants from seed is like any other kind of child-rearing. It is an arduous activity and not one to be treated casually. Take it seriously, and give your little ones an approximation of a healthy environment—or do them a favour and decide to adopt them at a later age.

Over the years, I've developed a reasonably inexpensive and effective method of growing plants from seed. I put my setup together by trial and error, but if I had to do it again, I could probably assemble it in about two hours. The first requirement is a four-tube fluorescent light bank. They're expensive to buy new but easily and cheaply obtained at an industrial wrecking yard. The other components you'll need are some lamp chain and an electrical cord. If your memory and attention span are at all spotty, you'll also need a small electric fan and a 24-hour timing switch.

Wire the unit (or get someone to do it for you), and hang it above the table where your seed trays are. Make sure the light tubes are about eight inches above the trays. Hook up the timer so that the lights are on 18 hours a day—the plants need that much artificial light to compensate for the lesser intensities involved. (Leaving the light on for 24 hours could damage such plants as tomato seedlings, which require a daily period of dark.) Place the fan so that it moves the air lightly across the trays. With the lamp chain, you can jack up the height of the light unit as the plants grow, maintaining the eight-inch distance. You don't need to buy those ridiculously expensive purple grow lights. A combination of warm white and cool white fluorescent tubes will get you essentially the same spectrum of light at a fraction of the cost.

If this sounds complicated, it is. But if you're determined to grow things indoors from seed, you'll need to take it at least this seriously. The store-bought equivalents of the unit I've described may be prettier, but they can be very expensive.

□ *SOME HELPFUL HINTS*

□ Don't crowd the seeds in your trays. Less seed usually results in more plants.
□ If you're recycling seed trays or plastic pots, make sure you sterilize them in a light bleach solution before use.
□ Avoid overwatering. It's often a good idea to set the flat with drainage holes inside another without holes so that excess water has somewhere to go.
□ Allow for good air circulation.
□ Read the instructions on seed packages before planting. Some seeds, like those of petunias, need darkness or warmth for germination. Others, like parsley, like to sit in the freezer for a few days before they are planted.
□ If your seedlings start to keel over, run 10 feet in one direction and then 10 feet in the opposite direction. Then go to your local nursery and buy something called No-Damp, a treatment for controlling the fungi that cause something called damping-off in germinating seeds. After transplanting your surviving seedlings to clean soil and reviewing which of the above approaches you may have neglected or overlooked, apply No-Damp. Some gardeners even use it as a preventive measure when they are preparing their soil for seeds.

□   *SEEDS: SORTING OUT AN ENIGMA*

Seeds are, in a phrase, a world of fun. They're also the building blocks of the garden, a source of disease and heartache and an uncertain realm in which there are few firm laws or truths except the one about sterile seeds not producing live plants. There is much more to seeds than the simple act of plucking packages of them off the rack at the local supermarket.

You can obtain seeds from your local plant nursery, or you can order them from seed catalogues. There are benefits and liabilities to both. Your local plant nursery will have seeds from a variety of commercial seed companies, which is an advantage—you can pick from among various selections offered by different companies. In recent years, a much wider choice of seeds has become available. If the staff are knowledgeable, they can supplement the information on the seed packages, which is usually minimal and frequently misleading or wrong. I try to buy my seed from the company that is closest to where I live. The reason? Seed produced locally will tend to be acclimatized to local conditions.

The seed catalogues, on the other hand, are great fun. When they arrive in late fall, they always provide a couple of evenings' entertainment—both in reading the silly testimonials they offer and in the more serious business of planning out next year's garden. If you are going to grow bedding plants from seed, the catalogues offer a distinct advantage, since the seed you order will arrive early in the new year. Your local nursery won't get its new seeds until considerably later.

The suitability and accuracy of seed catalogues are much more dependent

A late-summer garden with a variety of annuals in bloom: in front are pincushion flowers, with a range of different-coloured asters behind. Against the stone house grow cleome, also known as spider flower because of its airy, spidery shape.

on the companies' locations in relation to yours than the catalogues tend to admit. Seeds that come from zones very different from your own will perform badly. If it isn't possible to buy seeds from a nearby seed company, go to a good garden shop, one that won't sell you last year's seed. And remember not to believe everything seed companies say about their products, either in the catalogues or on seed packages.

I'm a great believer in collecting my own seed and in obtaining seed from my neighbours. It isn't just that I'm an amateur plant geneticist. Seed obtained from a neighbour is already adjusted to microclimatic variables and will therefore perform substantially better than seed from half a continent away.

Improving your own seed can also provide significant benefits. Be sure that what you're collecting isn't from a hybrid (the seed will be sterile) and that

it isn't from a species that can crossbreed with similar species (for instance, if you experiment with squash seeds, you might end up with something that resembles a pumpkin and tastes like an old zucchini). Beans are a good species with which to experiment, since they seem to conform better to Mendelian logic than most plants. Take seeds from the earliest specimen or from the most robust, or both. Like seems to beget like, and genetic anomalies most frequently appear late in a plant's life.

Storing seeds can be a problem because of their vulnerability to insect attack and fungi. I've solved the problem by storing my seeds in sealed jars along with packages of the desiccant used by electronics manufacturers in packaging for new equipment. Once the equipment is unpacked, the retailers don't have any use for the desiccant. Remember, I said you should improvise.

If only to keep this book from ending with a piece of advice about raiding electronics stores for free desiccant to prevent home-harvested seeds from getting mouldy, I owe you some sort of concluding statement that summarizes my approach to gardening. There's a certain appeal to just leaving it with that tip. If you follow it, it will have you rummaging around a deep-city alley attempting to recycle an inorganic type of industrial packaging—an almost unimaginable activity 30 years ago but, in the 1990s, the sort of thing we're all going to have to get better at doing.

Still, it lacks formal symmetry, and more important, practical tips aren't quite all I have in mind with this book. So, to that end, how about I wax philosophical about why I garden the way I do and why I wrote this book? You've probably already figured out that I'm not very interested in setting myself up as an expert on the subject of small-space gardening. I have another motive, and since about halfway through the writing of *The Compact Garden*, I've also had a secret title and subtitle: *The Off-the-Wall Gardener: A Nonexpert Gardening Approach to Civilization.*

When I'm not gardening or playing sandlot softball (the other amateur passion in my life and one that I've been involved in almost as long as gardening), I'm a journalist and a fiction writer. Nearly everything I've written has been a defence of the particularities of local culture, ecology and economics and against the homogenizing influence of what I call the Global Village. The term "Global Village" is my shorthand for the consumerist global economic system that is being imposed on North Americans and on the rest of the world in the name of efficiency and sound business practices.

I'm all for efficiency and sound business practices, and I'd be the first to recognize the need for a global community and for a planetary view of ecology, economics and culture. What worries me is that we're getting only the economic component of that necessary community. The Global Village is too nearsighted to be truly efficient, and by reducing our lives to a set of standardized consumer experiences, it reveals its own lack of vision. It believes that human reality is a bottom-line accounting balance sheet with a terminal point about 18 months in the future, and it is robbing us of the energies we need to protect ourselves, our cities, our planet and the democratic institutions that are our species' proudest achievements. Is that a sound business practice? I don't think so.

The 10 years I spent as an urban planner convinced me that democracy works best at the grass-roots level and that our ability to nurture, protect and enjoy the things and people around us will dictate the justice and effectiveness of our larger undertakings and concerns. Those are the things that the Soviet bloc forgot, and a quick look around our cities, with their growing crime rates, their faster-growing numbers of homeless people and their degenerating ecosystems, will provide us with ample evidence that we're forgetting the same things. The struggle to care for the specific against the onslaught of the generic, the rights and needs of the community against those of the opportunity-crazed individual—and the back garden against the plastic simplicity of Disney World or the consumer mall—is a political struggle we can't afford to lose.

A lot of my colleagues are surprised when they discover that I've been an active gardener since childhood. They are still more surprised that I'm writing a gardening book. Some have criticized it as silliness or a career step sideways. To me, it is a perfectly consistent and perhaps even an overdue move for me to make. My activities and attitudes as a gardener have generated and influenced my global concern as much as they've been informed by them. Gardening is not only a pleasant form of recreation, it is a *civilizing* thing to do, among the most effective and affective expressions of our understanding of civil life.

Having said all this, let me step down from my soapbox and summarize what I've had to say about compact gardens in terms with which gardeners will be more familiar: For the last 50 years, I think we have been relying too much on technical expertise to solve what are often really social dilemmas. We've been trying to create a large, logical world without bothering to pay attention to the specific and immensely complex organic components that make up individual and community life. We're doing it across our civilization, and we are doing it in our city gardening spaces. In so doing, we're thoughtlessly overlooking the most specific source of information and feedback available: our neighbours.

I'm not suggesting that we abandon technical expertise, but I am, at least in the garden, suggesting a fundamental shift in the way we approach both our pleasures and our difficulties. In crowded cities and confined spaces, our gardening ought to be less an expression of personal aesthetic ambitions and predilections and more an opening out into our surrounding cityscapes and our herbal and human neighbours. Whether we admit it or not, gardens are part of the political arena, and the way we garden reflects and influences our other values.

By using the approaches I've suggested in this book, we can start to become—as I've said elsewhere in several different ways—part of the solution, not part of the problem. We can also learn what the problems are in terms that are specific enough to grasp with our own hands. And our hands, filled with the rich loam we have helped to create, will be surer and more relaxed, making us better able to discover and share the ultimate purpose of life: to have—and make—fun.

☐ *CLIMATIC-ZONE MAP*

This simplified version of the U.S. Department of Agriculture's latest climatic-zone map indicates general temperature trends throughout Canada and the United States. The temperature ranges indicate average minimum winter temperatures. Colder zones have lower numbers. Nursery catalogues usually indicate the coldest zone in which a plant will thrive. Plants that are successful in your zone and in zones with numbers lower than yours should survive winters in your garden. Plants that prefer zones with higher numbers than yours may not be winter-hardy for you.

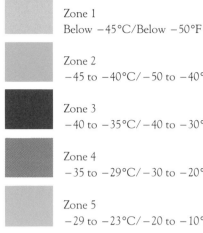

Zone 1
Below −45°C/Below −50°F

Zone 2
−45 to −40°C/−50 to −40°F

Zone 3
−40 to −35°C/−40 to −30°F

Zone 4
−35 to −29°C/−30 to −20°F

Zone 5
−29 to −23°C/−20 to −10°F

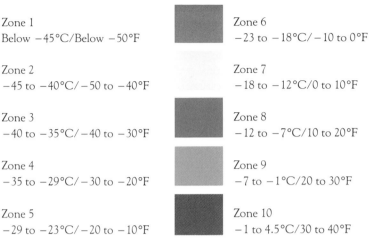

Zone 6
−23 to −18°C/−10 to 0°F

Zone 7
−18 to −12°C/0 to 10°F

Zone 8
−12 to −7°C/10 to 20°F

Zone 9
−7 to −1°C/20 to 30°F

Zone 10
−1 to 4.5°C/30 to 40°F

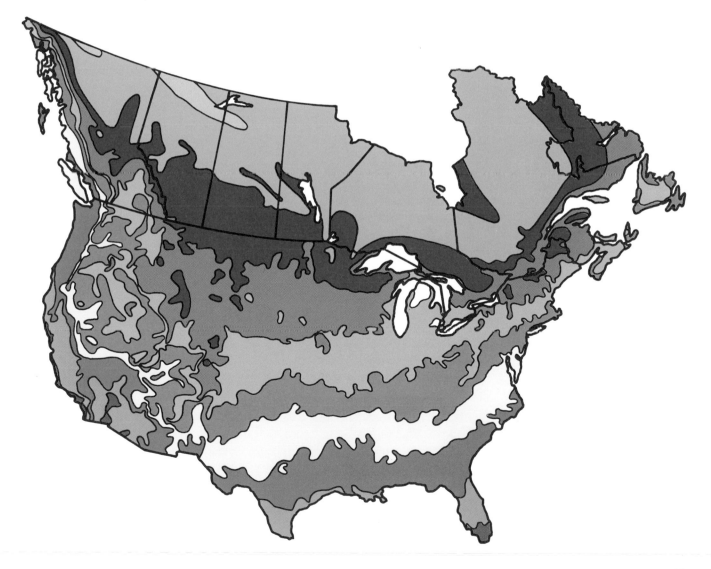

Seeds can be imported into either the United States or Canada without difficulty, but special arrangements are needed for living plants and plant materials. To import plant materials from the United States, Canadians must obtain a Permit to Import from the Permit Office, Plant Health Division, Agriculture Canada, Ottawa, Ontario K1A 0C6. Obtain one form for each nursery. To import plants from Canada, Americans must ensure that their purchases are accompanied by an invoice showing the quantity and value of the plants and a document from Agriculture Canada stating that the plants are free of diseases and insects. Canadian nurseries that accept U.S. orders routinely comply with these requests.

Alaska Yukon Plant and Seed Co.
Box 5499
North Pole, Alaska 99705
Short-season seeds and plants.

Alberta Nurseries & Seeds Ltd.
Bowden, Alberta T0M 0K0
Vegetables, herbs and flowers for cool and prairie gardens.

William Dam Seeds Ltd.
Box 8400
Dundas, Ontario L9H 6M1
Interesting selection of vegetables and flowers.

J.A. Demonchaux
827 N. Kansas Avenue
Topeka, Kansas
French seeds.

Dominion Seed House Ltd.
115 Guelph Street
Georgetown, Ontario L7G 4A2
All the essentials.

The Fragrant Path
Box 328
Fort Calhoun, Nebraska 68023
Seeds for fragrant plants.

Gardenimport inc.
Box 760
Thornhill, Ontario L3T 4A5
Imported bulbs, seeds and rare plants.

Gardens North
34 Helena Street
Ottawa, Ontario K1Y 3M8
Unusual and hardy perennials. Also annuals and biennials.

Grace's Garden
Autumn Lane
Hackettstown, New Jersey 07840
Novelty plant seeds.

Halifax Seed Co. Inc.
Box 8026, Station A
5680 Kane Street
Halifax, Nova Scotia B3K 5L8
Seeds for Atlantic gardens.

Horticultural Enterprises
Box 34092
Dallas, Texas 75234
Mainly pepper seeds and other hot items.

Japonica Nursery
Box 236
Larchmont, New York 10538
Japanese cultivars.

Johnny's Selected Seeds
Foss Hill Road
Albion, Maine 04910
Seeds for short-season climates.

Kitazawa Seed Co.
356 W. Taylor Street
San Jose, California 95110
Seeds for Oriental plants.

Lee Valley Tools Ltd.
Box 6295, Station J
Ottawa, Ontario K2A 1T4

McFayden Seed Co. Ltd.
Box 1800
Brandon, Manitoba R7A 6N4
All the basics in vegetable, flower and herb seeds.

Nichols Garden Nursery
1190 N. Pacific Highway
Albany, Oregon 97321
Rare vegetable and herb seeds.

Prairie Grown Garden Seeds
Box 118
Cochin, Saskatchewan S0M 0L0
Vegetables that grow successfully on the prairies.

Richters
Box 26
Goodwood, Ontario L0C 1A0
More than 300 culinary, aromatic and medicinal herb seeds and plants.

T&T Seeds Ltd.
Box 1710
Winnipeg, Manitoba R3C 3P6
Flowers and vegetables.

Thompson & Morgan Inc.
Dept. 125-2
Jackson, New Jersey 08527
A large number of new and unusual varieties.

Tsang & Ma International
Box 294
Belmont, California 94002
Seeds for Chinese plants.

The Urban Farmer
22000 Halburton Road
Beachwood, Ohio 44122
Seeds for dwarf plants.

Vermont Bean Seed Co.
Garden Lake
Bomoseen, Vermont 05732
Corn, beans and peas.

Vesey's Seeds Ltd.
York, Prince Edward Island C0A 1P0
Seeds for short-season gardens, all tested on the farm.

Dr. Yoo Farm
Box 290
College Park, Maine 04104
Seeds for Oriental plants.

RECOMMENDED READING

America's Garden Book, by James and Louise Bush-Brown. New York Botanical Garden and Scribner's, New York, 1980. A hefty classic originally published in 1939 and subsequently revised and updated. Offers "accessible and authoritative information about all of the important aspects of gardening." Sort of, anyway.

Better Vegetable Gardens the Chinese Way, by Peter Chan. Graphic Arts Center Publishing Company, Portland, Oregon, 1974. This book is intended for gardeners with larger gardens, but the principles are the same. The photographs are terrific.

Chatelaine's Gardening Book, by Lois Wilson. Maclean-Hunter, Doubleday, Toronto, 1988. A practical reference for Canadian gardeners, including information on how-to basics, garden types and descriptions of plant groups. Lists of recommended species and varieties for particular regions, purposes and sites are useful. A little suburban but okay.

The Complete Book of Edible Landscaping, by Rosalind Creasy. Sierra Club Books, San Francisco, 1982. A little too chic for my taste, but if you ignore that, you'll find it pretty useful.

The Complete Guide to Bulbs, by Patrick Synge. Dutton, New York.

Fruits and Berries for the Home Garden, by Lewis Hill. Knopf, New York, 1977.

The Gardener's Journal and Record Book, by E. Annie Proulx. Rodale, Emmaus, Pennsylvania, 1983. A helpful if somewhat squirrelly organizational manual and resource book.

Grow Your Own Chinese Vegetables, by Geri Harrington. Collier, New York, 1978.

Growing Good Roses, by Rayford Clayton Reddell. Harper and Row, New York; Fitzhenry & Whiteside, Toronto, 1988. Informative, sensible and entertaining, this easy-to-read guide includes advice on buying, planting, maintaining and exhibiting modern garden roses. I'd rather phone my father, but since he won't let me give you his telephone number, this will do.

The Harrowsmith Annual Garden, by Jennifer Bennett and Turid Forsyth. Camden House, Camden East, Ontario, 1990. As practical, readable and informative as its companion, *The Harrowsmith Perennial Garden*, this takes an in-depth thematic look at annuals suited to a range of garden situations and gardeners' interests. Useful even for a very small garden.

The Harrowsmith Book of Fruit Trees, by Jennifer Bennett. Camden House, Camden East, Ontario, 1991. Particularly sensitive to northern dreamers. Packed with information on every aspect of cultivating fruit trees in the home garden and includes experts' choices of species for particular regions.

The Harrowsmith Perennial Garden, by Patrick Lima. Camden House, Camden East, Ontario, 1987. Informative throughout, the book begins with start-up and design basics, acknowledges the challenges of northern gardening and looks at perennial gardening in each of the growing seasons. Useful book.

Plants for Dry Climates, by Mary Ross Duffield and Warren D. Jones. HP Books, Tucson, Arizona, 1982.

Reader's Digest Illustrated Guide to Gardening in Canada. Reader's Digest Association, Montreal. Best Canadian book, elegantly and intelligently illustrated. Only occasionally inaccurate.

Rodale's Color Handbook of Garden Insects, by Anna Carr. Rodale, Emmaus, Pennsylvania, 1979. For those who like really gruesome pictorial information on the little buggers devouring their gardens.

Soil Processes, by B.J. Knapp. Allen & Unwin, London, 1979. Written from a British perspective but not location-specific.

Spring Flowers: A Harrowsmith Gardener's Guide, edited by Katharine Ferguson. Camden House, Camden East, Ontario, 1989. Covers the growth habits and planning, planting and care requirements of spring-flowering bulbs, perennials and shrubs. Technical but useful.

Square Foot Gardening, by Mel Bartholomew. Rodale, Emmaus, Pennsylvania, 1981. Based on the PBS television series, this book has errors and tends to be overmeticulous. Bartholomew is far too fond of planting marigolds, but if you want to get serious about vegetable productivity and can ignore the crunchy granola tone, this book is very useful.

10,000 Garden Questions Answered by 20 Experts, edited by Marjorie Dietz. Doubleday, Garden City, New York, 1982. Seems more like 100,000 questions are answered in its 1,500 pages of questions and answers. A wonderful book.

Tottering in My Garden, by Midge Ellis Keeble. Camden House, Camden East, Ontario, 1989. A book to come back to again and again, not just for the down-to-earth "Notes for the Novice" or the practical, learned-from-experience advice, but for the good sense and good humour we are invited to share as we romp (tromp) through 40 years — and six gardens — of Keeble's life.

p. 3 Rosalind Creasy
p. 8 Tim Saunders
p. 9 Tim Saunders
p. 10 Lefever/Grushow/Grant
  Heilman Photography
p. 13 Karen Bussolini
p. 14 Jane Grushow/Grant
  Heilman Photography
p. 17 John Neubauer
p. 20 Peter Bennett
p. 23 Jerry Pavia
p. 24 Rosalind Creasy
p. 25 Rosalind Creasy
p. 26 Beth Powning
p. 33 Peter Bennett
p. 34 Walter Chandoha
p. 41 Lefever/Grushow/Grant
  Heilman Photography
p. 42 Walter Chandoha
p. 46 Rosalind Creasy
p. 47 Walter Chandoha
p. 49 Lefever/Grushow/Grant
  Heilman Photography
p. 50 Walter Chandoha
p. 55 Turid Forsyth
p. 56 Walter Chandoha
p. 58 Larry Lefever/Grant Heilman
  Photography
p. 63 Rosalind Creasy
p. 66 Edward Lee/Tony Stone
  Worldwide/Chicago Ltd.
p. 71 Walter Chandoha
p. 72 Rosalind Creasy
p. 74 Malak Photographs Ltd.
p. 75 Gay Bumgarner/Tony Stone
  Worldwide/Chicago Ltd.
p. 76 Rosalind Creasy
p. 79 Kathlene Persoff
p. 80 Rosalind Creasy
p. 83 Kathlene Persoff
p. 84 John J. Smith
p. 88 Derek Fell
p. 91 Grant Heilman/Grant
  Heilman Photography
p. 92 Rosalind Creasy
p. 95 Cosmo Condina/Tony Stone
  Worldwide/Chicago Ltd.
p. 96 Lefever/Grushow/Grant
  Heilman Photography
p. 100 Lefever/Grushow/Grant
  Heilman Photography
p. 102 Lefever/Grushow/Grant
  Heilman Photography
p. 108 Steve Terrill
p. 111 John J. Smith
p. 113 Wolfgang Kaehler
p. 114 Derek Fell
p. 116 Malak Photographs Ltd.
p. 119 John Scanlan